The Young Eyewitness

The Young Eyewitness

**How Well Do Children
and Adolescents
Describe and Identify
Perpetrators?**

Joanna Pozzulo

American Psychological Association
Washington, DC

Published by
American Psychological Association
750 First Street, NE
Washington, DC 20002
www.apa.org

To order
APA Order Department
P.O. Box 92984
Washington, DC 20090-2984
Tel: (800) 374-2721; Direct: (202) 336-5510
Fax: (202) 336-5502; TDD/TTY: (202) 336-6123
Online: www.apa.org/pubs/books
E-mail: order@apa.org

In the U.K., Europe, Africa, and the Middle East, copies may be ordered from
American Psychological Association
3 Henrietta Street
Covent Garden, London
WC2E 8LU England

Typeset in Minion by Circle Graphics, Inc., Columbia, MD

Printer: Maple Press, York, PA
Cover Designer: Minker Design, Sarasota, FL

The opinions and statements published are the responsibility of the authors, and such opinions and statements do not necessarily represent the policies of the American Psychological Association.

Library of Congress Cataloging-in-Publication Data

Names: Pozzulo, Joanna, author.
Title: The young eyewitness : how well do children and adolescents describe
  and identify perpetrators? / Joanna Pozzulo.
Description: Washington, DC : American Psychological Association, [2017] |
  Includes bibliographical references and index.
Identifiers: LCCN 2016003648 | ISBN 9781433822926 | ISBN 143382292X
Subjects: LCSH: Child witnesses—United States. | Forensic child
  psychology—United States.
Classification: LCC KF9673 .P69 2017 | DDC 363.25/8—dc23 LC record available at
  http://lccn.loc.gov/2016003648

British Library Cataloguing-in-Publication Data
A CIP record is available from the British Library.

Printed in the United States of America
First Edition

http://dx.doi.org/10.1037/14956-000

This book is dedicated to Jessica and Emma,
the best nieces an aunt could have.

Contents

The Young Eyewitness

Introduction

In the neighborhood park, children are swinging from the monkey bars and pushing to get their turn on the slide, laughing and enjoying the warmer weather that spring brings. Parents chat with each other while a 7-year-old boy goes off to look for rocks so he can build a fort with his friends. A man approaches the boy and asks whether he needs any help. The youngster says no. The man then asks whether the boy is hungry and would like a chocolate bar. When the boy says no, the man attempts to grab the boy and lift him into his arms. The boy starts screaming and frees himself from the stranger's hold, running back to the other children and adults. The stranger runs off. How accurate a description of the stranger would the young boy and the other children provide? For that matter, would the adults provide similar descriptions as the children? Would the children (and adults) be able to identify the stranger from a lineup?

http://dx.doi.org/10.1037/14956-001
The Young Eyewitness: How Well Do Children and Adolescents Describe and Identify Perpetrators?
by J. Pozzulo

Every year, numerous abductions, murders, thefts, and other crimes occur in which children are victims of and/or witnesses to the crime (e.g., Finkelhor, Turner, Ormrod, Hamby, & Kracke, 2009). For example, in one survey with a large nationally representative sample of children (ages 1 month–17 years) and their caregivers, approximately three in five children had been exposed to at least one act of violence either as a victim or a witness in the prior year (including physical assault, sexual victimization, maltreatment, property victimization, and witnessing violence; Finkelhor, Turner, Shattuck, Hamby, & Kracke, 2015).

In some cases, children are the only witnesses to a crime, so forensic investigators cannot corroborate the children's statements with adult eyewitnesses' statements. In such cases, investigators must rely on the children to describe the event, describe the perpetrator, and sometimes identify the perpetrator from a lineup. But how reliable is this evidence? How complete or accurate are a child's responses to interview questions? Because of their unique developmental status, children and adolescents may be less able to recall an event, describe a perpetrator, and identify him or her in a lineup. They may "remember" incorrect information about what happened or how the perpetrator appeared. They may even identify an innocent person as the perpetrator.

When we examine known cases of wrongful conviction, we notice the frequency with which eyewitness evidence was erroneous and contributed to unjust outcomes. Given the devastating outcomes that can accompany erroneous eyewitness evidence—including incarceration and capital punishment—it is imperative that we understand the young eyewitness's descriptive and identification abilities and the factors and conditions that can increase or decrease their accuracy. And that is the aim of this book.

This volume summarizes research on children's and adolescents' abilities to recall an event, describe a perpetrator, and identify him or her, as well as the conditions that optimize these abilities. Although young eyewitnesses tend to be less advanced in these skills than adults, they can still provide valuable evidence. The key intended audience for the book includes forensic investigators and those who evaluate eyewitness evidence, because these people must understand how both the nature of the crime and the conditions of the subsequent interview and lineup affect the completeness and accuracy of young people's responses.

Several exceptional sources are available elsewhere delineating the strengths and weaknesses of adults' eyewitness descriptions and identifications (Brewer & Wells, 2011; Cutler & Kovera, 2010; Malpass, Ross, Meissner, & Marcon, 2009; Wells & Olson, 2003). Thus, that topic is not reviewed herein unless it helps with understanding children's eyewitness abilities.

The chapters that follow describe the conditions and procedures that can increase (and decrease) the likelihood of a young eyewitness providing accurate evidence. To give background and context for this review, Chapter 1 first provides real-world examples of crimes that involved a young eyewitness and then defines key terms and concepts for understanding research in this area. Chapter 2 reviews the recall ability of young eyewitnesses, and Chapter 3 suggests techniques to improve this ability. Chapters 4 and 5 review the identification ability of young eyewitnesses. Chapter 6 considers why young eyewitnesses' abilities might differ from adult eyewitness abilities, and Chapter 7 considers whether there is any relationship between young eyewitnesses' recall ability and their identification ability. Chapter 8 reviews the research on how jurors perceive young eyewitnesses, including the perceived reliability of children's interview responses and testimony. Chapter 9 considers policy implications, and Chapter 10 suggests new directions for research in this area.

It is my hope that readers gain a fuller understanding of the value of child eyewitness evidence, as well as ways to maximize that value when interviewing these children.

1

Overview of Forensic Concepts

Knowing research terminology and concepts is important for understanding this volume, but so is being aware of the broad context of crimes involving child eyewitnesses. Lest we lose sight of this context, I begin this chapter by providing several real-world examples of crimes involving young eyewitnesses, including the conditions that were present, the procedures police used to elicit the description and identification of the perpetrator from the young eyewitnesses, and the outcome of the cases. The examples collectively show that although child eyewitness statements are sometimes unreliable, they can also provide the information necessary to solve cases.

After the examples, I define and describe some key forensic concepts and terms to help you understand the literature presented in the following chapters. Included are precise forensic definitions of *recall, recognition,*

http://dx.doi.org/10.1037/14956-002
The Young Eyewitness: How Well Do Children and Adolescents Describe and Identify Perpetrators?
by J. Pozzulo

suspect, perpetrator, and *target* and a discussion of basic study designs that are used to research these topics.

REAL-WORLD EXAMPLES OF CHILD EYEWITNESSES

In choosing the cases, I attempted to select a cross-section of eyewitness ages to cover the span of the "young eyewitness," geographical location (restricted to cases in the United States), and police procedures used. The eyewitness most often is the victim, but not in all cases. Some of the cases received much media attention, whereas others are less well known. In some cases, we know the accuracy of the outcome, whereas in others we do not. The cases provide a context for the scientific research that is reviewed in the following chapters and are used for illustrative purposes. These cases highlight the nature of descriptions and identifications of perpetrators by the young eyewitness and how they are perceived in court. The evidence is at times accurate and other times inaccurate. In some of these cases, we simply do not know the veracity of the evidence provided by the young eyewitnesses. What is clear is that young eyewitnesses can provide compelling evidence that has value in a court of law.

Mary Katherine Smart (Witness)[1]

Fourteen-year-old Elizabeth Smart was taken from her family home early in the morning of June 5, 2002. Her sister, Mary Katherine (9 years old), with whom she shared her bedroom, was in her bed that night and was the sole eyewitness to the abduction. Mary Katherine reported that a man entered their room sometime in the middle of the night. She watched as he quietly woke Elizabeth and forced her out of her bed, threatening that he would kill her and her family if she did not quickly get up and follow him. Mary Katherine witnessed that the man led Elizabeth to the bathroom (which was connected to the closet) to get shoes and that they then left down the hall. Mary Katherine attempted to warn her parents but

---

[1] Case information for this section was obtained from ABC News ("Sister Recounts," 2005), CBC News (Associated Press, 2011), McFarland and Falk (2010), Morgan (2011), Moses (2010), and *United States of America v. Mitchell* (2010).

became frightened when she saw that the man and Elizabeth were still in the hallway. She went back to her bed and pretended to sleep for several hours before she alerted her parents.

Mary Katherine later testified that the man who abducted her sister was holding a knife (although early reports stated that she thought it was a gun) and was wearing light clothing. However, later testimony provided by Elizabeth revealed that Mitchell was dressed in dark clothing, including sweat pants, a sweat shirt, tennis shoes, and a stocking cap. Mary Katherine did not recognize the man, although she stated that his voice sounded familiar. The sisters' mother, Lois, told a reporter that police had asked her not to discuss the abduction with Mary Katherine for fear that Mary Katherine's memories would be tainted by others' recollections or suggestions. Immediately after the abduction, Mary Katherine moved in with her grandparents, where she stayed for several months. In fall 2002, Mary Katherine moved back into her family home, although it took some time before she was able to sleep in her bedroom again. In October 2002, Mary Katherine was in her room, the room where the abduction occurred, looking through a *Guinness World Records* book when the name Emmanuel popped into her mind. She then claimed that Emmanuel was the abductor.

Emmanuel was a transient who had been hired to do odd jobs for the Smart family several months before the abduction. Mary Katherine testified that she had first encountered Emmanuel in the fall of 2001 when she was school shopping with her mother and siblings. After that meeting, Emmanuel was hired by the Smart family to do some odd jobs around the home. Mary Katherine could not recall directly speaking with Emmanuel while he was working at her family home; however, she remembered being present during a conversation that her brother had with him. A sketch of Emmanuel based on Mary Katherine's description was created and made public by the television program *America's Most Wanted*. As a result, Emmanuel was identified as Brian David Mitchell, and numerous tips were received by the hotlines regarding his location.

In March 2003, 9 months after Elizabeth was abducted, police received a tip from a concerned citizen who had seen *America's Most Wanted* that Mitchell was walking with two unidentified females wearing robes. Police stopped Mitchell on the side of a road, where he was with two females,

Wanda Barzee and Elizabeth Smart. Elizabeth was rescued, and Mitchell and Barzee were taken into custody. Mitchell was found guilty and sentenced nearly 9 years after Elizabeth's abduction. It took prosecutors this long to obtain a conviction because Mitchell, although deemed competent for trial by a federal court, had his proceedings delayed twice by a state judge who ruled that Mitchell was unfit for trial because of mental illness. It was at this last trial that Elizabeth first addressed Mitchell directly. She had previously testified at Mitchell's trials; however, Mitchell would often have to be removed from the court for disrupting the proceedings by singing.

Mitchell received two life sentences at his hearing in Salt Lake City, Utah, and was charged in the state court system with six other felonies, including aggravated kidnapping, aggravated sexual assault, and aggravated burglary. Wanda Barzee pleaded guilty to federal kidnapping and received a 15-year sentence in a federal prison hospital in Texas for her role in the abduction. Elizabeth took the stand to confront her abductor, stating, "I have a wonderful life. . . . You will never affect me again" (Associated Press, 2011, para. 9).

Lori Poland (Victim–Witness)[2]

On Monday, August 22, 1983, at approximately 12:45 p.m., 3-year-old Lori Poland was playing outside near her house in Sheridan, Colorado, when she was abducted. Her father was inside their house and had told her to stay close by, and her mother was at work. Lori's friend who had been playing with her informed Lori's mother that a man approached Lori, asked her whether she wanted to go for ice cream, told her to take off her pants, and insisted she get into his car. This friend and a nearby resident were among those interviewed by Sergeant Louis Florez of the Sheridan Police Department, and they indicated that the abductor was a White man driving a yellow/brown/burnt orange Datsun with black side stripes and a license plate number containing ADV-2. Local media were almost immediately contacted for assistance.

---

[2] Case information for this section was obtained from Associated Press (1988), Betts and Chatman (1984), Goleman (1984), People v. Thiret (1984), Rowland (2005), the Spokane Chronicle ("Abducted Child Found," 1983), and The Bulletin ("Kidnapped Child," 1983).

Soon after the abduction, 22-year-old Robert Paul Thiret was identified as a suspect by the appearance of his car. Thiret had allegedly approached a 5-year-old girl approximately 6 weeks before abducting Lori, and the girl's father, Stanley Ellis, had seen Thiret's vehicle and recorded the license plate number. After he had learned about Lori's abduction, Ellis called the police with this information. On August 23, 1983, Thiret's home was searched, and he was questioned by both the police and the FBI. Thiret claimed he had been napping during the time of the abduction; however, his car had been left running in the driveway with the keys in the ignition. On August 24, Robert Sexton, an investigator with the district attorney's office, asked Thiret where he would look for a missing person, and Thiret suggested Bear Creek Park. Ultimately, Thiret's appearance did not match the description provided by witnesses to the abduction, and Thiret passed a polygraph test. He was therefore released. However, his car was impounded.

On August 25, 1983, a couple of birdwatchers, Steven and Cynthia Gaulin, were hiking 15 miles west of Denver in Stapleton Park. After using an outhouse, they heard a child crying for help. They began to search the vicinity of the outhouse and heard the child cry "Mommy." Using a flashlight, the Gaulins peered underneath the outhouse floor into the 10-foot deep pit. They spotted young Lori, wearing only her underpants. When they asked her why she was there, she replied, "I live here." After being rescued, she cried and clung to her rescuer, fearful of being returned to the pit. She said her abductor had hit her for crying and left her in the hole. She was taken to the hospital, where she was reunited with her parents. She had to spend some time in intensive care because of circulation and infection problems in her feet.

On August 26, 1983, Thiret's house was searched again, and his vehicle was returned. Hairs from his vehicle were found to match Lori's hair. The next day, Lori was presented with a 12-man lineup and audibly gasped as she identified Thiret. She told police, "That one: He did it. He put me in the hole. He was mean. He was a bad guy" ("Kidnapped Child," 1983, para. 3). When Lori was shown a lineup without the suspect in it, she asked where his picture had gone. On August 29, Lori was shown another lineup with Thiret in it and again positively identified him. She was released from the hospital on August 30.

On September 1, 1983, police searched Thiret's house again. On September 7, Thiret was arrested for attempted first-degree murder and second-degree kidnapping. Bail was set at $250,000. Thiret maintained his innocence. Further charges of sexual assault and child abuse were filed against Thiret on September 12. It was discovered that Thiret had been contacted five times in the prior 8 years regarding matters of a sexual nature. Lori's ability to identify the defendant as her abductor was challenged by Thiret's public defender, Craig Truman. He also objected to the recordings, both audio and visual, that had been made of Lori being interviewed by police and a medical doctor. The judge decided that Lori would not have to identify Thiret in court. Instead, she was allowed to identify him from a lineup for the court before the trial commenced on March 7, 1984. There were further arguments by Thiret's attorneys that the search of Thiret's property and car were done too quickly without proper procedures, but the rebuttal for this was that it was not known at the time of the first search whether Lori was even alive—time was of the essence.

On September 26, 1984, a week before his case was to go to trial, Thiret pled guilty to attempted murder and sexual assault and received a sentence of 10 years. The reasoning for this sentence was that some of the evidence had been declared inadmissible, and the prosecutor was not confident that a guilty verdict could be obtained. In December 1990, Thiret was released, with no parole conditions, after serving only 6 years of his sentence. He is now a registered sex offender.

In February 1998, Lori was awarded the Metropolitan Mayors and Commissioners Youth Award, for overcoming adversity. In May 1998, Lori graduated from high school, having been chosen as both homecoming queen and prom queen. In May 2003, she graduated from college.

Brooke Sutton (Victim–Witness)[3]

In June 1998, 6-year-old Brooke Sutton was sleeping at her 58-year-old grandmother's house in Summit County, Ohio, after attending a birthday

---

[3] Case information for this section was obtained from *Elkins v. Summit County Ohio* (2010), Farkas (2006), the Innocence Project (n.d.), Leung (2009), Possley (n.d.), Ramsland (n.d.), and Reiselman (2006, 2013).

party. During the night, Brooke's grandmother, Judith Johnson, was first beaten, then strangled to death and subsequently raped. Brooke also was beaten and sexually assaulted and then strangled until she lost consciousness and was left for dead.

When Brooke woke up several hours later, she discovered that her grandmother had been murdered. She left a telephone message for a friend, later presented as evidence, in which she said, "I'm sorry to tell you this, but my grandma died, and I need somebody to get my mom for me. I'm all alone. Somebody killed my grandma" (James, 2007, para. 19). In her bloody nightgown, she left her grandmother's house and found a neighbor at home. The neighbor asked Brooke to wait outside for approximately half an hour while she finished making breakfast for her children. The neighbor then drove Brooke home. At the time, nobody asked why Brooke was forced to wait outside or why the neighbor had not called the police. Furthermore, the neighbor was the first person to say that Brooke identified her attacker as Brooke's Uncle Clarence.

Brooke's parents immediately drove her to get medical help. At the hospital, Brooke expressed some doubt as to whether her attacker was actually her uncle. However, she then decided that it definitely had been her uncle who had committed the crimes. Police wrote down this statement. She also reiterated this information to the medical professionals and her relatives.

Within hours of the crime, Clarence Elkins, Brooke's uncle, was arrested. Elkins provided an alibi, supported by his wife, that he had been home sleeping at the time of the crime. However, Elkins and his wife were not sleeping in the same bed. Police believed that Elkins could have left the house without his wife's knowledge, despite the wife's insistence that her dog would have barked if Elkins had gone out.

During Elkins's 1999 trial, Brooke again identified Elkins as her attacker. This was the sole piece of evidence that incriminated him, but it was persuasive enough to lead to his conviction of rape and murder. Elkins received a life sentence for these crimes.

Four years after her attack, now 10-year-old Brooke recanted, claiming Elkins had not been her attacker. She also provided new information about the crime, such as the fact that her attacker had been wearing western-style boots. In addition, she now claimed that her attacker's eyes had been brown, whereas Elkins's eyes were blue. Her recantation led to Elkins's lawyers' request for a new trial. However, a request for a new trial at this time was not granted for the reasons that Brooke had obtained the information about her attacker's eye color through hypnosis, which might have distorted it, and that her family members at a recent family reunion had likely been applying pressure and had coached her to recant her testimony.

The Ohio Innocence Project took on Elkins's case in 2004 on the basis of the facts that there was no physical evidence linking Elkins to the crime and that he had no prior criminal record. Extensive DNA analysis demonstrated that the DNA found on Brooke's underwear and under her grandmother's fingernails and in her vagina had come from one male only and that this male was definitely not Elkins. Despite this evidence, a motion for a new trial by the Ohio Innocence Project was denied because Elkins had not been convicted on the basis of DNA evidence, but rather on Brooke's eyewitness identification of him. Elkins appeared to be doomed to spend the remainder of his life in prison.

However, the Ohio Innocence Project was soon made aware by Clarence's wife, Melinda Elkins, of a new suspect. Melinda Elkins had never stopped fighting for her husband's freedom and had recently started to look further into the suspicious behavior of the neighbor Brooke had gone to immediately after the attack. She discovered that the neighbor's live-in boyfriend at the time of Brooke's attack, Earl Mann, had since been convicted and was serving time for raping three young girls.

On January 5, 1999, during the Elkins trial, Mann was arrested by Barberton police for two robberies. During his arrest, Mann, who was intoxicated, asked patrol officer Gerard Antenucci, "Why don't you charge me with the Judy Johnson [Brooke's grandmother] murder?" Antenucci claimed to have written an "interdepartmental memorandum" containing Mann's statement, which he placed in a mailbox that was to be emptied each day by a member of the detective bureau. This memorandum was never disclosed or presented during Elkins's trial.

In a strange twist of fate, Elkins was transferred not only to the same prison but also to the exact cell block that Mann was in. Elkins managed to retrieve a cigarette butt that Mann had stubbed out in a clean ashtray. Elkins sent this to his lawyer in a contraband Ziploc bag. Mann's DNA from the cigarette was found to match that obtained from Judith Johnson and from Brooke. Even though Mann's DNA was found to be a match, the district attorney still did not allow Elkins to be released from prison. The Attorney General for Ohio, Jim Petro, held a press conference to convince Elkins's prosecutor to drop the charges against him. One more test of the DNA was performed to reconfirm Mann's guilt, after which Elkins was released from prison on December 15, 2006. Elkins ultimately received a settlement of approximately $1 million from the State of Ohio for his wrongful imprisonment. In June 2007, Mann was indicted for the rape and murder of Johnson. In 2008, Mann pled guilty and was sentenced to 55 years to life.

Elkins was the Ohio Innocence Project's first exoneration. Fueled by the Elkins case, a new Ohio Innocence Protection Act was enacted. This act has been referred to as a national model, consisting of best practices for eyewitness identifications, rules for preserving DNA, and incentives for police officers to record their interrogations.

Kathy Sigman (Witness)[4]

December 3, 1957, was a day that started like any other but ended in tragedy for Maria Ridulph. Maria was a 7-year-old girl who was playing outside with her friend Kathy. A man, referring to himself as "Johnny," came up to the girls and asked whether they wanted piggyback rides. Maria agreed, but Kathy had to run home to grab something, and when she got back, Maria and Johnny were nowhere in sight. Kathy went and told her mother that the nice man named Johnny was the last person she saw Maria with. Maria's dad reported her missing later that evening. Police and local neighbors searched for any sign of Maria and spotted one of Maria's dolls next to the garage where 18-year-old John Tessier (who, years later, went by the name Jack Daniel McCullough) and his parents lived.

---

[4] Case information for this section was obtained from A. O'Neill (2013), *People v. McCullough* (2012), and Ward (2012, 2015).

Police questioned Tessier's parents about his whereabouts. The mother stated that he had been out of town that night, a lie.

During the police investigation, Kathy spent many hours at the police station and was shown numerous mug shots of ex-convicts; however, she did not see Johnny. The best evidence the police had was 7-year-old Kathy's story. Some of the details varied (e.g., at what time she came back outside and found Maria and Johnny gone), but she never wavered on the core facts: He "wore a striped sweater of blue, yellow and green. He had long, blond hair that curled in the front and flopped onto his forehead" (O'Neill, 2013, para. 62). Police received an anonymous tip that the description of the perpetrator sounded like a man named "Treschner" who lived in the neighborhood and was 18 years old at the time of the crime. They again ended up at the Tessier residence. John Tessier's parents still claimed that their son had nothing to do with Maria's disappearance.

Maria's body was found in the spring of the following year. The body was so badly decomposed that there was no way to obtain any DNA. When questioned, Tessier said that he remembered the little girl as being "stunningly beautiful with big brown eyes" (O'Neill, 2013, "Lovely, Lovely, Lovely," para. 3). Tessier's alibi was that he was not in town the night of the abductor, that he was on his way to Chicago. Police found the train ticket stub that was good for 30 days; however, the ticket had never been used. Tessier also said that he stopped at his girlfriend's house that night for a date; his girlfriend stated that she never saw him that night. Last, Tessier said that he was with a classmate on the search team for Maria; this friend said that was not true, and he never saw him. Tessier passed a lie detector test, and the FBI's expert concluded that a teenager would not have been able to conceal his involvement in this crime. There was no tangible evidence to convict Tessier. His name was then taken off the list of possible suspects. The case went cold.

Fifty-three years later, there was a knock on Kathy's front door. The Illinois State Police had reopened the case when they received a tip. The tipster said her mother knew who was responsible for Maria Ridulph's disappearance and murder: the tipster's half-brother, John Tessier, who now resided in Seattle, Washington. "John did it" (O'Neill, 2013, "Hearsay Rulings: 'I'm Toast,'" para. 7), his mother admitted on her deathbed.

The police reopened the case and wanted to show Kathy another lineup. Six mug shots were presented to Kathy simultaneously (see Figure 1.1), and among these photos was a picture of Tessier. Kathy eliminated several photos right away, but she continued to glance over two—numbers one and four. After studying them for a couple of minutes, she finally chose photograph four. "That's him," she said (O'Neill, 2013, "Chapter 4: 'That's Him,'" para. 23). She did not know whose picture she had chosen. "I couldn't forget that face," she later recalled (O'Neill, 2013, "Chapter 4: 'That's Him,'" para. 26).

Seattle police tracked down the man in the photograph, who now went by the name Jack Daniel McCullough (formerly known as Johnny). At first, McCullough came across as though he had no concerns. He made small talk and joked with the officers. The officer showed him the lineup photos of the suspects in the case. In the number four spot was the photo of him, which Kathy had identified. McCullough avoided looking at it. He studied the photographs and stated that he did not recognize any of them (not even the one of himself). He finally agreed that picture number four

Figure 1.1

Lineup used that included McCullough (#4). Court exhibit retrieved from http://www.cnn.com/interactive/2013/08/us/oldest-cold-case/evidence.html. In the public domain.

was of him, but that it was "a very poor picture," and he did not recognize himself (O'Neill, 2013, "Lovely, Lovely, Lovely," para. 18). Kathy was resolute on the witness stand while she recounted the story she had told so many times before: how a friendly stranger who called himself Johnny offered them piggyback rides. She recounted how Maria and Johnny were gone when she returned from a quick trip home to grab her mittens. Kathy stood her ground when she was shown the same six photos of suspects she had seen in years prior. She was firm in her conviction that she had identified the right person and without hesitation went straight to the fourth picture from the left: "This photo right there," she said, tapping the picture of McCullough (O'Neill, 2013, "Staring Down 'Johnny,'" para. 6).

McCullough waived his right to a trial by jury, opting instead to have his case heard by a judge. Jack Daniel McCullough was found guilty of the murder of Maria Ridulph at age 73, 55 years after the crime had been committed. He was sentenced to life in prison. America's longest standing cold case was finally solved. Since then, McCullough has filed a motion for a new trial; however, that motion has been denied.

On October 12, 2012, in his motion for a new trial, McCullough claimed that the six photographs failed to provide a fair, unbiased, and reliable photographic lineup. McCullough claimed that his photograph did not show a gap between his teeth as in the description of the suspect given to the FBI, and he found his photograph suggestive for the following additional reasons:

- All five filler photos had a white background, whereas the defendant's photo had a black background.
- In all five filler photos the men were wearing suits and ties, whereas the defendant was wearing different clothing.
- In all five filler photos the men were looking slightly to the right in a yearbook style pose, whereas the defendant was staring directly into the camera.
- In all five filler photos the men had neatly combed hair, whereas the defendant had unruly hair.
- The defendant's photo had an amateur quality that caused his ear to shine brightly in the picture.

- All five filler photos were taken directly from a yearbook, whereas the defendant's was not.

McCullough remains in prison.

Kendra Lewis (Witness)[5]

In the early morning hours of August 5, 1992, gunshots were fired. Three people were outside an apartment building and saw 4-year-old Kendra Lewis run out. Kendra ran to three people and said, "Dre just shot my mama's eye out" (*Mancill v. State*, 2001, para. 1). When the police arrived on the scene, they found Kendra's mother, Yolanda Lewis, lying on the bed and another man, Ace Johnson III, lying behind the front door. Each victim had been shot twice in the head with the same gun. Kendra Lewis was questioned at the scene by the police officers, and she told them that "Dre shot my mama." She then said, "There go Dre," while pointing out Durwyn Mancill, also known as Deandre Jones, while he was walking down the street with his friends (*Mancill v. State*, 2001, para. 1). Mancill was indicted on November 10, 1992.

At trial, Kendra testified, "Andre killed my mother with a big gun, hurting her in the head" (*Mancill v. State*, 2001, para. 1). She also testified that she saw Johnson get killed "on the front door" (*Mancill v. State*, 2001, para. 1). The police presented Kendra with a six-person photo lineup that included Mancill and two other suspects in the case. Kendra pointed out "Andre" (Mancill); furthermore, she identified the defendant as Andre when she turned around to face him. She was not able to identify another suspect who was brought into the conference room during her testimony.

During the trial, two videotaped interviews of Kendra were shown to the jury. The testimony given in these videos was consistent with the testimony presented at the trial. In the first videotape Kendra volunteered, "My mama got killed" and "Andre killed her" in response to a preliminary question about who brought her to the interview (*Mancill v. State*, 2001, para. 3). Kendra had identified "Dre" as the shooter to bystanders

---

[5] Case information for this section was obtained from *Chatman v. Mancill* (2006) and *Mancill v. State* (2001).

immediately after the murders and pointed out Mancill to police as he walked down the street that morning. In addition to the testimony of the eyewitness, other witnesses testified that Yolanda Lewis had dated Mancill. Mancill testified in his own defense and said that he was sleeping with friends in the living room of an apartment in a different building when the shootings occurred. Mancill's defense was that another man named Dre, either one of Johnson's associates or Lewis's former boyfriend, committed the murders. After a trial lasting 2½ weeks, he was convicted of the two murders and the trial court on April 19, 1993, imposed two life sentences. He continues to plead his innocence for the murders.

Unknown Child (Victim–Witness)[6]

On November 15, 2004, a 9-year-old was walking home from the school bus stop when she was grabbed from behind. The abductor placed his hand over the child's mouth and told her that he had a knife. The child then kicked the abductor in the shin, and he eventually let go and released her. Once released, the child turned around and "poked the abductor in the eye repeatedly for about twenty seconds" (State v. Guard, 2013, para. 1). The child and abductor struggled until the child ultimately broke free and ran toward home, noticing that the abductor was running in the opposite direction when she turned to look back.

When she reported the incident to her mother, the mother and the child went out to look for the abductor but did not find him. Her mother then called the police. When asked by police, the child described the abductor as

> a male who was wearing white shoes, jeans, and a hat with curly hair sticking out from underneath. She also claimed that the abductor could have been Hispanic and had a shadow of a mustache or beard but that she did not get a good look at his face. (State v. Guard, 2013, para. 3)

After speaking to a detective with more experience and training in interviewing children, the child described the suspect as tall, taller than the offi-

---

[6] Case information for this section was obtained from State v. Guard (2013).

cer but shorter than the detective, approximately 5'7" to 6'1" tall. She also described him as being slightly overweight. Further into the interview, the child gave a more specific description of the abductor's clothing, describing the hat as "a black baseball cap with the letter 'A' on it and claiming that he wore tennis shoes and a black 'Stone Cold' Steve Austin t-shirt" (*State v. Guard*, 2013, para. 3). When the child was asked whether she would recognize the abductor if she saw him again, she acknowledged that she would. At trial, the child's testimony was consistent with the description she provided to police, with the exception of the color of the abductor's shoes (she told the police the shoes were blue, but on cross-examination she clarified that his shoes were white).

A schoolmate who got off at the bus stop with the child corroborated the child's description of the abductor's clothing, describing the abductor as wearing a hat, blue pants, a black shirt, and white shoes. She also confirmed that the abductor grabbed the child, let go, and then ran in the opposite direction from the child.

The child was asked to view a six-photograph lineup that included a photograph of Jimmy D. Guard.

> All the men used to construct the lineup had short dark hair, dark complexions and were slightly overweight however Guard was the only man to have curly hair and no facial hair as opposed to four other members of the lineup who did. (*State v. Guard*, 2013, para. 4)

The child viewed a sequential lineup: She was presented with each photograph individually and asked to identify the man who tried to abduct her. The child eliminated the first two photographs of the lineup, stating, "No, that's not him" (*State v. Guard*, 2013, para. 4). When the third photograph, the one of Guard, was presented, the detective testified that "her eyes got big, she appeared excited and scared at the same time and she immediately said, 'That's him. That's him. Yes, I'm sure that's him'" (*State v. Guard*, 2013, para. 4). The child also testified that she "was a hundred percent" positive of the identification while eliminating the remaining members of the lineup (*State v. Guard*, 2013, para. 4).

Two witnesses also provided information regarding the time of the crime. One neighbor stated that she thought she saw Guard run past her house between 3:15 and 3:45 p.m. while she was waiting for her children to come home from school. A second neighbor claimed that he thought he saw someone who resembled Guard waiting at a Utah Transit Authority bus stop for approximately half an hour; however, the man did not board the bus when it arrived at 3:00 p.m. The second witness stated that the man began to follow three girls once they got off the school bus but that he did not see any of them being grabbed. When police obtained a search warrant for Guard's home, their search revealed none of the clothing described by the child, apart from a pair of blue running shoes.

Guard was found guilty of child kidnapping; however, he appealed on the basis of the court's decision to exclude an expert eyewitness testimony about the reliability of eyewitness identification. The Court of Appeals of Utah vacated Guard's convictions, and he was "remanded for a new trial in accordance with this decision" (*State v. Guard*, 2013, para. 28).

KEY TERMS AND CONCEPTS

To understand the research summaries in the following chapters, a critical distinction has to be made between the terms *suspect* and *perpetrator*. A *suspect* is a person who the police suspect committed a crime. A suspect may or may not be guilty of the crime in question. Thus, a suspect may or may not be the perpetrator. In contrast, a *perpetrator* is the guilty person who committed the crime. The term *target* refers to the person who has to be described or identified—in other words, the target is the perpetrator.

Recall and *recognition* refer to memory processes. *Recall* occurs when one is describing the perpetrator and/or details of the crime; recall is likened to an essay-style exam question in which you are asked to state all that you can remember as it relates to the question being asked. In contrast, *recognition* occurs when one identifies (from a lineup or photographs) the perpetrator who committed the crime; recognition is likened to a multiple-choice exam question in which one must select the correct answer from the options provided. Thus, when describing a perpetrator or the crime, we are engaging recall memory; when identifying a perpetrator, we are engaging recognition memory.

RESEARCHING FACE RECOGNITION:
BASIC STUDY DESIGN

Research on facial recognition draws heavily from *signal detection theory*, which seeks to explain how well and under what conditions people can distinguish relevant information (also known as the *signal* or *stimulus*) from irrelevant information (also known as *noise*). In facial recognition studies, the target face is the signal, whereas the other individuals' faces are the noise.

In studies of face recognition, participants are exposed to a series of faces through the use of photographic materials, usually in a slide presentation and, now, on a computer monitor. Participants may or may not be told to remember the faces or be given specific instructions on what to do when a face appears (e.g., decide whether the face is male or female). Once all the faces have been presented, participants may have an intervening task that is unrelated to the faces previously seen. For example, participants may have to work on math problems for a short time (e.g., 15 minutes). Then participants are presented with another set of faces containing the previously shown faces interspersed with new faces. Participants must decide which faces are "old" (i.e., previously seen; in the terminology of signal detection theory, these faces are the signals) and which faces are "new" (i.e., not seen before; in the terminology of signal detection theory, these faces are noise). Responses are coded according to two fundamental criteria: (a) whether there was a signal present and (b) whether the participant responded that there was a signal present. Four outcomes are possible:

- A *hit* indicates that the participant responded "yes" when there was a signal present.
- A *miss* indicates that the participant responded "no" when there was a signal present.
- A *false alarm* indicates that the participant responded "yes" when there was no signal present.
- A *correct rejection* indicates that the participant responded "no" when there was no signal present.

RESEARCHING LINEUP IDENTIFICATION: BASIC STUDY DESIGN

To study lineup identification, participants are exposed to an event (e.g., staged theft) without their prior knowledge and, in particular, without warning that they will later have to identify the target/confederate. This unawareness is created to mimic the real-world unexpectedness of crime. The event may be seen live or shown by slides or videotape/DVD. For example, a confederate steals a professor's bag in front of a class, and students in the class then become eyewitnesses. Typically, there is only one person for the eyewitness to identify. The participants are asked to describe what occurred and to describe the perpetrator. A delay between the event and lineup test may or may not be imposed. The delay could be the amount of time it takes to describe the event and person (e.g., 15 minutes vs. 1 hour) or it can be longer when the participant–witness is asked to return the next day (or later).

For the identification phase, a small set of photographs is shown (often six), only one (or even none) of which may be the perpetrator. Two types of lineups are used: target-present lineup and target-absent lineup. A *target-present lineup* contains a photo of the perpetrator (in different clothing to ensure *person identification* rather than recognition of the picture) and a set of fillers, distractors, or foils, usually five others who are similar in appearance to the perpetrator. Three kinds of decisions are possible with this type of lineup:

- *Correct identification* occurs when the witness identifies the guilty suspect; this can only occur with a target-present lineup. A correct identification is the only correct decision with a target-present lineup.
- *Foil identification* occurs when the witness incorrectly identifies a known-to-be innocent lineup member. A *foil*, also known as a *distractor*, can appear in a target-present or target-absent lineup.
- *False rejection* occurs when the witness states that the perpetrator is not present in a lineup when in fact the perpetrator is present, and the suspect is guilty. This can only occur with a target-present lineup.

A *target-absent lineup* is created when a similar-looking substitute for the perpetrator is included, and the same five foils from the target-present lineup are included as well. Three kinds of decisions are possible with this type of lineup:

- *Correct rejection* occurs when the witness states that the perpetrator is not present in a lineup when in fact the perpetrator is absent, and the suspect is not guilty. This can only occur with a target-absent lineup. A correct rejection is the only correct decision with a target-absent lineup.
- *Foil identification* occurs when the witness incorrectly identifies a known-to-be innocent lineup member. (This also occurs with a target-present lineup.)
- *False identification* occurs when the witness states that the suspect is guilty when in fact the suspect is innocent. This can only occur with a target-absent lineup.

Table 1.1 summarizes the possible decisions with a target-present versus target-absent lineup.

Last, a distinction must be made between system variables and estimator variables (Wells, 1978). *System variables* are those variables that occur after the crime that can influence an eyewitness's accuracy. Such variables include interview protocol and lineup procedure. *Estimator variables* are present at the time of the crime and cannot be controlled or changed after

Table 1.1

Possible Decisions as Functions of Target Presence Versus Absence

	Correct identification	Foil identification	False rejection	Correct rejection	False identification
Target-present	✓	✓	✓	X	X
Target-absent	X	✓	X	✓	✓

Note. ✓ = Indicates the decision is possible; X = Indicates the decision is not possible. Shaded areas indicate the only accurate decision possible.

the fact. Such variables include age of the witness, race of the perpetrator, and amount of time spent viewing the perpetrator. This volume examines both system and estimator variables.

These terms appear throughout the volume, and understanding the distinctions will aid in the comprehension of the material that follows. The terms will not be repeated in the following chapters but rather will be expanded on.

CONCLUSION

The cases in this chapter demonstrate that it can be difficult to determine the accuracy of child and adolescent descriptions and identifications. But this evidence can nonetheless be invaluable in solving cases, finding missing persons, and bringing perpetrators to justice. The following chapters examine the scientific evidence regarding descriptions and identifications to gain a fuller understanding of the conditions under which descriptions and identifications of a young eyewitness are more or less likely to be accurate. Readers may refer to this chapter as needed to review key definitions and concepts for forensic research.

2

Ability of Young Eyewitnesses to Describe a Person

Consider the following description provided by a 16-year-old girl who claimed to have been abducted and assaulted at gunpoint while walking to school one morning ("Barrhaven Sexual Assault," 2011). The girl described her abductor as a male in his 40s, about 5'6", light brown or olive skinned, speaking English with a French accent, with a slightly protruding stomach and dark, shaggy, ear-length hair. He was wearing a beige suede coat, blue jeans, black work boots, glasses with thin black rims, and a gold wedding band. He was driving an older, red, four-door SUV with winter tires, no hubcaps, and no front license plate. The car had two front bucket seats, but the rear seats had been removed. Are you struck by the number of details she provided? A key difference between this description and those highlighted in Chapter 1 is the number of details and the level of detail. In this particular case, a few days following the investigation, the 16-year-old recanted her allegation and reported that she had fabricated

http://dx.doi.org/10.1037/14956-003
The Young Eyewitness: How Well Do Children and Adolescents Describe and Identify Perpetrators?
by J. Pozzulo

the assault and all the details. This is not to say that a detailed description is obviously inaccurate; certainly there are descriptions that can be very detailed and contain accurate information.

When we examine the descriptions found in the case studies in Chapter 1, we see that the amount of information provided by a child witness can vary greatly. The six case studies that were summarized in Chapter 1 illustrate a commonality often observed in descriptions of perpetrators, namely, that they are brief. Moreover, the information or details provided often apply to many and in some cases do not match the suspect's or perpetrator's appearance.

This chapter focuses on the abilities of young eyewitnesses to describe a perpetrator. It also provides an overview of the nature of descriptions provided by the young eyewitness in terms of what details are reported, the quantity of those details, and their accuracy. Last, this chapter explores whether the person descriptions provided by young eyewitnesses should be relied on by the criminal justice system.

Overall, few studies have systematically investigated perpetrator descriptions. Fewer studies have examined descriptions of perpetrators provided by young eyewitnesses and how these descriptions compare with those provided by adult eyewitnesses. What we know about perpetrator descriptions tends to come from two sources: archival reviews of real-life cases and laboratory studies. Both sets of research are discussed here.

PERSON DESCRIPTIONS BY YOUNG EYEWITNESSES

How do we "assess" the young eyewitness's ability to describe a stranger? In several studies, a target engages with participants on a task, such as mask making, for a brief period (20 minutes or so), and then the target exits and participants are asked to describe the target. Often the participants are questioned individually with broad-based questions (e.g., "What did Sally look like?"), and the researcher notes what the participant says. Young eyewitnesses who are a bit older (e.g., 9 years and older) and adults will often be asked to write down what they remember about the target.

This information is then coded to determine the nature, quantity, and accuracy of person descriptions.

A Note on Coding

The information obtained pertaining to person descriptions comes in the form of qualitative information that must be coded or scored in some manner; the method used can influence the number and accuracy of descriptors presented in result sections of published papers. Typically, a rubric is established before scoring descriptions based on the target's appearance. It is not uncommon for two independent scorers to score a percentage of the descriptions (e.g., 20% of the total). Coefficients will be calculated to determine the agreement between the coders. Discrepancies are often discussed, and a decision is made on how to code the item. The entire process continues until there is sufficient agreement between the coders (e.g., approximately 80% of the items are coded similarly). Of course, researchers may use different methods for coding. There also is software available, such as NVivo, to code unstructured data (see http:// www.qsrinternational.com/what-is-nvivo). The method used will affect what is reported, and it is difficult to compare studies, given all these differences. The data discussed later in the chapter must be interpreted cautiously when comparing studies and, for that matter, when comparing studies with real-life case examples.

A Note on the Target

Inherent differences across targets, such as distinctiveness, may influence the nature, number, and accuracy of descriptors reported. For example, consider a target with distinctive hair—it is likely that the number of descriptors would be focused on this feature and may include several descriptors about hair that would not come up in another study that used a target with less distinctive hair. This difference could suggest that young eyewitnesses provide numerous descriptors; however, it may be more a function of the target than the young eyewitness's ability. Without studies using more than one target, it is difficult to draw conclusions across studies. Again, we must be cautious in our generalizations.

Young Eyewitnesses' Ability to Describe a Target

Keeping these cautions in mind, few descriptors are provided by young eyewitnesses (and adult eyewitnesses). Some studies have found that very young eyewitnesses (5–6 years old) can report one or two descriptors, children in middle childhood (8–12 years old) can report a few more, and adults can report a few more than that. The number of descriptors reported is not straightforward and is dependent not only on the age of the eyewitness but also on other factors, such as how the information is obtained (i.e., what questions are asked to elicit the descriptions). (For a more thorough discussion of techniques to obtain descriptive information, see Chapter 3.) Moreover, the methodology used, such as whether the target was seen live or on video, may influence the descriptors reported and the accuracy of the descriptors. Even when studies use a live target to reach their conclusions, we still should be careful when generalizing to the real world. Witnesses to actual crime may fear for their life or may have witnessed a traumatic event, such as having a caregiver murdered, as in the case of Kendra Lewis, who witnessed her mother being shot to death (see Chapter 1). It is difficult to gauge how these factors may affect eyewitness descriptions (and identifications). Next, a few studies are described highlighting a cross-section of ages and methodology and the impact of these on the nature, quantity, and accuracy of person descriptions.

Examining the abilities of preschoolers (3–6-year-olds), Pozzulo, Dempsey, and Crescini (2009) had the youngsters engage in a 20-minute mask-making session conducted by a female confederate who acted as the mask-making teacher. Following a delay of about 20 minutes after the mask-making session ended, a researcher asked preschoolers individually to describe the mask-making teacher. On average, preschoolers reported 1.57 person descriptors, with 58% mentioning hair color. Clothing color was mentioned 47% of the time, followed by hair length, with 20% mentioning it, and clothing type, with 17% mentioning it. Other descriptors that were mentioned included height (7%), complexion (6%), eyes (1%), body type (1%), and accessories (1%). Some preschoolers also mentioned nonphysical descriptors, such as disposition and actions.

Also using a live target, Davies, Tarrant, and Flin (1989) elicited descriptors of a target from younger (6–7 years) and older (10–11 years) children. Each child was seen by one of two male confederates posing as "health survey researchers," who recorded the child's weight, height, and eye color. The following week, the children were interviewed individually and asked to describe the confederate they had seen during the previous week's encounter. The children were asked to describe features such as hair, face shape, eyes, mouth, nose, and the male's age. The interviewer would ask several questions about each feature (e.g., "What was the color of hair? Thickness? Length? Straightness?"). When asked to simply describe the man (i.e., free recall method), younger children reported fewer descriptors, with only one person descriptor on average, than older children, who reported 2.21 person descriptors on average. However, when prompted with cues such as "Tell me about their hair color," younger children seemed to recall just as many descriptors as older children (11.99 and 11.64, respectively).

Examining descriptors provided by middle-aged children, Zajac and Karageorge (2009) had 8- to 11-year-old children visit a local police station. Partway through the visit, a male confederate entered the room, asking the police officer running the session whether he could borrow keys to the jail cells. The police officer handed the confederate several keys fastened by a ring. Children were exposed to the confederate for approximately 45 to 60 seconds. Children were interviewed 1 day after the session at the police station. During the interview, children were asked for a verbal description of the confederate. They were given prompts such as "Can you tell me anything else about him?" until the children stopped providing details. On average, children provided 2.97 descriptors. Zajac and Karageorge found that children were most likely to give hair descriptors (given by 83% of participants), followed by clothing descriptors, physical descriptors (e.g., "tall," "accent"), facial descriptors, and finally, age descriptors, with only 2% of children reporting age.

In a follow-up study that expanded the age range of child witnesses, Karageorge and Zajac (2011) had children ages 5 to 7 years and 8 to 11 years briefly view a confederate for 30 to 45 seconds during a staged event at a fire station. After a delay of either 1 to 2 days or 2 weeks, children described the confederate using an open-ended format. Specifically, the interviewer asked the child, "Can you tell me what the man who slid down the fire pole looked like?" If children replied positively, the interviewer then gave minimal and neutral encouragement to continue (e.g., "Can you tell me anything else about the man who slid down the fire pole?") until children stopped providing information. Overall, most children provided 2.47 descriptors, and only five children provided more than four descriptors. The researchers found that the age of the witnesses interacted with the amount of delay. With the short delay of 1 to 2 days, there was no difference between the two age groups regarding the number of descriptors provided, with younger and older children reporting 2.48 descriptors on average. When the delay was longer, lasting 2 weeks, younger children reported 1.92 descriptors, significantly fewer than older children, who reported 2.78 descriptors on average. Children in either age group were most likely to report clothing, with 86.8% of children mentioning at least one clothing descriptor. Clothing was followed by hair (58.9%), face (14.0%), "other" (12.4%), and age (7.0%) descriptors.

Using a videotape methodology, Pozzulo, Dempsey, Crescini, and Lemieux (2009) examined children's and adults' person descriptive abilities across two studies. In Study 1, participants were shown a video of a staged purse theft at a university. In this study, children (M_{age} = 10.25) reported significantly fewer person descriptors (M = 6.67 descriptors) than did adults (M_{age} = 21.73; M = 10.21 descriptors). In Study 2, a different staged crime involving a purse theft in a food court was used. Again, children (M_{age} = 10.35; M = 4.25 descriptors) reported significantly fewer person descriptors than did adults (M_{age} = 20.92; M = 10.38 descriptors).

As discussed in Chapter 1, Mary Katherine (9 years old) noted a weapon and light-colored clothing when first describing her sister's abductor. The description Kathy Sigman (7 years old) gave included the color of the abductor's sweater, in addition to hair length, color, and style (i.e., "long, blond hair that curled in the front and flopped onto his forehead"; O'Neill,

2013, para. 62). Thus, there is variability in the number of details reported, although hair and clothing seem to be two categories often mentioned. Again, it is important to keep in mind that how details are coded can influence the number of details a researcher concludes are reported. For example, describing hair as short, blonde, and straight can be coded as three items or as one item, "hair."

For older children, Pozzulo and Warren (2003) conducted two studies that varied the gender of the target and the type of exposure (video exposure vs. live exposure) to the target for child witnesses ages 10 to 14 and adult witnesses. In Study 1, child and adult witnesses saw a video of a male target discussing "street-proofing" (i.e., strategies on how to stay safe) for approximately 1 minute. Participants were given an open-ended description form and asked to write down everything they remembered about the target's appearance. Young eyewitnesses reported significantly fewer descriptors, an average of 7.61 descriptors compared with adults, who reported 9.85 descriptors on average. The researchers speculated that if the descriptors were separated into broad categories (e.g., exterior face descriptors, interior face descriptors, body descriptors, clothing descriptors, accessory descriptors, and "other"), there may have been a difference in the amount of information recalled in some categories by young eyewitnesses compared with adult eyewitnesses. Indeed, young eyewitnesses reported significantly fewer descriptors than adults across three categories: exterior face descriptors such as hair length and style (1.71 vs. 2.22 descriptors), interior face descriptors such as eye color (1.00 vs. 2.38 descriptors), and body descriptors such as weight (0.97 vs. 1.35 descriptors). Conversely, adults reported significantly fewer accessories such as jewelry (0.05 descriptors) than young eyewitness (0.16 descriptors). When it came to clothing, young eyewitnesses and adults reported a similar number of descriptors. Thus, these young eyewitnesses reported either fewer or a similar number of descriptors than did adults.

In a second study that used a live target, Pozzulo and Warren (2003) examined young eyewitnesses (10–14 years old) and adult eyewitnesses. In small groups of participants, the female target provided a brief introduction to the study. Participants saw the target for approximately a minute. After about 20 to 25 minutes, participants were asked to write down everything they remembered about the target. Young eyewitnesses reported significantly fewer descriptors than did adults, with an average of 3.64 compared with 8.09 descriptors for young eyewitnesses and adults respectively. Compared with adults, young eyewitnesses reported significantly fewer descriptors across almost all categories (except for "other").

Examining the adolescent eyewitness, Pozzulo, Dempsey, and Pettalia (2013) used a videotaped mock crime and compared adolescents (M_{age} = 16.49 years) with young adults (M_{age} = 20.16 years). Participants completed a free recall description form following the viewing of the videotaped staged crime of a male perpetrator stealing a woman's bag at a bus stop. Witness age was not found to influence the total number of descriptors recalled. Adolescents recalled 7.58 descriptors on average, whereas adults recalled 7.69 descriptors on average. When descriptors were divided into broad categories—total exterior face items, total interior face items, total body descriptors, and total clothing descriptors—adolescents and adults produced a similar number of descriptors across category. See Table 2.1.

For more studies that examined the young eyewitness and the number of descriptors reported as a function of age, see Table 2.2 and Table 2.3. The studies have been divided by type of methodology used to see the target, that is, video versus live viewing.

Table 2.1

Means (SD) of Descriptors as a Function of Type of Descriptor and Witness Age

Descriptor category	Adolescents	Adults
Exterior face	1.66 (.99)	1.62 (1.10)
Interior face	.41 (.79)	.41 (.65)
Body	1.39 (.93)	1.57 (.95)
Clothing	4.13 (3.80)	4.08 (2.40)
Total	7.58 (3.80)	7.69 (3.50)

Note. From "The Z Generation: Examining Perpetrator Descriptions and Lineup Identification Procedures," by J. D. Pozzulo, J. Dempsey, and J. Pettalia, 2013, *Journal of Police and Criminal Psychology*, 28, p. 68. Copyright 2013 by Springer. Adapted with permission.

Table 2.2
Total Number of Person Descriptors Provided in Studies Involving Child Eyewitnesses Viewing a Video

Study	Age of eyewitnesses	No. of person descriptors
Pozzulo, Dempsey, Crescini, & Lemieux (2009), Study 1	M_{age} 10.25 years	6.67
Pozzulo, Dempsey, Crescini, & Lemieux (2009), Study 1	M_{age} 21.73 years	10.21
Pozzulo, Dempsey, Crescini, & Lemieux (2009), Study 2	M_{age} 10.35 years	4.25
Pozzulo & Warren (2003), Study 1	10–14 years	7.61
Pozzulo & Warren (2003), Study 1	Adult	9.85
Pozzulo, Dempsey, & Pettalia (2013)	M_{age} 16.49 years	7.58
Pozzulo, Dempsey, & Pettalia (2013)	Adult	7.69

Table 2.3
Number of Person Descriptors Provided in Studies Involving Child Witnesses Viewing a Live Confederate

Study	Age of eyewitnesses	No. of person descriptors
Davies, Tarrant, & Flin (1989)	6–7 years	1.00
Davies, Tarrant, & Flin (1989)	10–11 years	2.21
Pozzulo, Dempsey, & Crescini (2009)	3–6 years	1.57
Pozzulo & Warren (2003), Study 2	10–14 years	3.64
Pozzulo & Warren (2003), Study 2	Adult	8.09
Zajac & Karageorge (2009)	8–11 years	2.97
Karageorge & Zajac (2011), 1–2 day delay	5–7 years	2.48
Karageorge & Zajac (2011), 1–2 day delay	8–11 years	2.48
Karageorge & Zajac (2011), 2 week delay	5–7 years	1.92
Karageorge & Zajac (2011), 2 week delay	8–11 years	2.78

ACCURACY OF DESCRIPTORS

Now that we have a general sense of the number and type of person descriptors provided by the young eyewitness, it is important to ask a critical question: How accurate are those descriptors? Although the young eyewitness may provide fewer person descriptors than the adult eyewitness, even young children can be highly accurate (e.g., Cohen & Harnick, 1980; Marin, Holmes, Guth, & Kovac, 1979; Roebers & Schneider, 2001). For instance, Marin et al. (1979) had participants ages 5 to 22 take part individually in a study in which they were interrupted three different times: once by the experimenter, once by the experimenter's assistant, and once by a male confederate. The participants' memories of the events were then examined through free recall, questioning, and a photo identification task. Participants returned 2 weeks later for another memory assessment for the same event. Ultimately, Marin et al. found that although children from ages 5 to 7 provided significantly fewer descriptors than did adults, they seldom volunteered false information and were as accurate as adults in answering objective questions and in their photo identifications. In fact, the youngest age groups provided false information significantly less often than did the other age groups. It is important to keep in mind that although adults recalled more, they also made more errors.

Karageorge and Zajac (2011) found that child eyewitnesses (5–7 years and 8–11 years) produced overall accuracy rates of 0% to 100% with an average accuracy rate of 70%. More than half (68%) of all descriptors were accurate. There may be an assumption that those who provide few descriptors have poor memories and are unlikely to be accurate. This assumption may not be accurate, however, especially when we consider the many factors that can influence the reporting of descriptors, such as linguistic ability. Karageorge and Zajac found that the number of descriptors reported was not related to the accuracy of the descriptors. Forty-three percent of the children were completely accurate in their descriptions. On the flipside, 11.6% of children were completely inaccurate with their descriptors. Most of the children provided descriptions that contained more accurate items than inaccurate items. The children were most accurate when providing descriptors related to age (78% accurate) and hair (76%), followed by clothing (67%) and face items (61%). The least accurately described category of descriptors (38% accurate) related to the "other" category, which included, for example, piercings and jewelry. Overall, there was an increase in accuracy as a function of age, with the older children providing more accurate descriptors ($M = 1.81$ descriptors) than did younger children ($M = 1.38$ descriptors).

In contrast to these results, Pozzulo and Warren (Experiment 2, 2003) found that for the most part, young witnesses ($M = 12.5$ years) were less accurate than adults ($M = 18.89$ years). Specifically, young witnesses were less accurate than adults when reporting body descriptors ($M_{accuracy} = .27$ vs. .60), clothing descriptors ($M_{accuracy} = .27$ vs. .43), and interior face descriptors ($M_{accuracy} = .17$ vs. .33). Young adults were as accurate as adults when reporting exterior face descriptors ($M_{accuracy} = .86$ vs. .85), accessory descriptors ($M_{accuracy} = .07$ vs. .11), and "other" descriptors ($M_{accuracy} = .05$ vs. .06). Consistent with results in Experiment 1 of the same study, young witnesses had difficulty with body descriptors and interior face descriptors. Inconsistent with their previous results, young witnesses were less accurate when describing the target's clothing than were adults. These differential results may have occurred because, with a live target, young witnesses may have become distracted by the target's words and actions, thus restricting the amount of attention available to observe the target's clothing and leading to a reduction in accuracy. It is difficult to be certain of this, however.

Pozzulo et al. (2013) examined the accuracy of descriptors for adolescents ($M = 16.49$ years) and young adults ($M = 20.16$ years). Accuracy was not found to differ, with one exception when considering the descriptor category of exterior face items (e.g., hair color, hairstyle): Adults were more accurate when describing exterior face items ($M_{accuracy} = .85$) than were adolescents ($M_{accuracy} = .61$).

Using cases involving real crime, Wagstaff et al. (2003) examined statements provided by 48 female victims, from 8 to 92 years old. These females were victims of single-perpetrator rape, attempted rape, or indecent assault who had provided a description of the perpetrator to at least one police officer. All data had been taken from cases in which the perpetrator had been subsequently apprehended after the crime. Furthermore, all cases were instances in which the crime involved only one victim or witness and in which the victim gave full statements, including descriptions of the offender's age, height, build, hair color, and hairstyle. The descriptions provided by the witness were coded by two raters, cross-referencing the descriptions with photographs of the actual perpetrator using a Likert-type scale ranging from very accurate to very inaccurate. Both hair color and hairstyle were classified using four categories (e.g., one category would consist of "brown," "dark," and "dark brown" for hair color and "short," "straight," "wavy," "curly," or "frizzy" for hairstyle) and build using three categories. Findings revealed that hairstyle and hair color of the perpetrator was recalled most accurately. Neither the level of violence, the presence of a weapon, nor age had a significant influence on reporting accuracy. The one exception to this finding was that reporting the perpetrator's hair color was more accurate with higher levels of violence (for rape).

Intriguingly, when we examine the recall literature more broadly—that is, the literature that involves recall for an event—a general finding is that children report fewer details than adults, but children are as accurate as adults (Jack, Leov, & Zajac, 2014). This finding appears to mirror the work with young eyewitnesses and adult eyewitnesses when describing a target. Although descriptions provided by young eyewitnesses may be briefer than those of adults, they may not be less accurate, and as such, police may be able to use these descriptions in their investigation of cases and apprehension of the perpetrator.

A Note on Reporting the Perpetrator's Age

The age of a perpetrator is often estimated to be in a range that can span 5 or 10 years, if not more. Young eyewitnesses may be at a disadvantage when estimating age, in that some research has suggested that estimating age outside one's cohort is more difficult than estimating the age of someone within one's cohort (Rhodes & Anastasi, 2012). Younger eyewitnesses would be at a disadvantage in estimating age in that the perpetrator is often outside a young eyewitness's cohort (e.g., a 6-year-old eyewitness vs. 20-year-old perpetrator; see Chapter 1 for examples of these age differences). Children may be prone to overestimating a target's age. For example, in February 1990, a 7-year-old girl was raped and left for dead. The victim, although accurate in many other details and able to identify the perpetrator from a lineup, described her attacker as being in his 30s or 40s when he was 24 years old (Ceci & Bruck, 1995, p. 16). In fact, Dent (1991) found that age was the most inaccurate descriptor provided by children. In a review, Ellis (1992) discussed the difficulties children appear to have when estimating the age of a person. His prior studies (Ellis, 1990, 1991) looked at how children of varying ages performed at facial identification when faced with facial transformations. All children tested had difficulty matching faces of the same person at different ages. Children aged 5 to 7 found it particularly hard, but the children ages 8 to 11 also had a lot of difficulty. Ellis suggested that this is likely due to their lack of personal experience in seeing people age over a long period.

A Note on Reporting the Perpetrator's Height and Weight

Children may have difficulty estimating weight and height (Davies & Flin, 1988; Davies, Stevenson-Robb, & Flin, 1988; King & Yuille, 1987), even though adults make errors with these descriptors as well (Flin & Shepherd, 1986). If the perpetrator is seen on media (e.g., videotape, computer screen, photographs), estimating weight and height can be challenging because it is difficult to use environmental markers (if there are any in the scene) to help with the estimate. Consider: How tall are doorways? Seeing someone in a doorway could be used to estimate height, but you would have to know how tall a doorway is. And of course, not all doorways are the same height. Even if a confederate/perpetrator is seen "live," it can be hard to estimate height. Adults may be able to use themselves as a reference point (e.g., I'm 5'9" and he was a little taller than me, so he's probably about 5'11".), but that can be even more difficult for children given (a) the larger gap between the height of a child and an adult versus the height difference between two adults and (b) children may not know how tall they are.

Being able to estimate weight accurately requires some notion of the relation between height and weight; that is, taller people are heavier than shorter people of similar girth. Children may have a harder time estimating these relations. As with height, an adult can use her- or himself as a reference for a weight estimate, but this is much more difficult for children, given their smaller stature and the fact that they may not know their own weight. Again, if the target is seen on media, weight can be even more challenging to estimate, given distortions that may occur due to the technology used. Estimating weight with live targets may be easier than if they are on a "screen," but it remains difficult.

Why Are so Few Descriptors Recalled by the Young Eyewitness?

Providing a free recall description is a verbal task that may be hindered by the fact that children's linguistic ability is less developed than that of adults. Children may have an inability to articulate the information they have stored and can remember. Alternatively (or in addition), children may encode fewer person details than do adults, limiting the number of descriptors that can be recalled and reported. Furthermore, children may focus on peripheral details, hindering their ability to report central person descriptors. Overall, there are many possibilities for why children may recall fewer descriptors than adults, and in all likelihood, there may be several combined reasons for why this occurs.

CONCLUSION

The young eyewitness tends to provide few descriptors when describing a "target." Descriptors tend to focus on hair, such as color and length, as well as on clothing, such as the color of the person's shirt. However, these details can vary depending on a number of factors, such as the distinctiveness of the target. It is important to keep in mind that the details provided by the young eyewitness, although few, can be accurate. The veracity of the details may be affected by how the information is solicited from the young eyewitness. Chapter 3 focuses on techniques used with the young eyewitness and their effectiveness in obtaining accurate descriptor information.

3

Techniques to Improve the Amount and Accuracy of Recall Information

The case summaries in Chapter 1 and the information on person descriptions provided by child eyewitnesses in Chapter 2 show that young (and adult) eyewitnesses provide police with little descriptive information, both in terms of quantity and in the distinctive details that can differentiate between many individuals. To facilitate the apprehension of the correct perpetrator, police need techniques that will allow witnesses to provide more complete and accurate person information. I review some of the techniques available to police in this chapter. These techniques, however, were not designed specifically to increase the amount and accuracy of person descriptions but rather to elicit more accurate information about event narratives (when the alleged perpetrator may be known). For the most part, the techniques used to increase person information are the same techniques used to increase memory for other details of the crime, such as action details (i.e., what occurred). Few techniques are geared specifically

http://dx.doi.org/10.1037/14956-004
The Young Eyewitness: How Well Do Children and Adolescents Describe and Identify Perpetrators?
by J. Pozzulo

toward eliciting information about the perpetrator's appearance—a limitation with some of these techniques. Nonetheless, these techniques provide some direction in eliciting as much accurate information as possible.

FREE RECALL

When asking children to recall details, police can use an open-ended approach (e.g., "Tell me everything you remember"). This style of questioning, without specific prompts that incorporate details that may or may not be accurate, allows the witness to respond with whatever information comes to mind. When this approach is taken, children's reporting is as accurate as the reports provided by adult eyewitnesses (Ceci & Bruck, 1993). Unfortunately, children tend to report little information. For example, when asked, "What did he look like?" a child may respond with, "He had brown hair." With very young eyewitnesses, say 3 and 4 years old, the response may be even further truncated to "Brown hair." Consider the number of potential suspects that have brown hair. If police want to narrow down the suspect pool with an eyewitness's description, they require more than a hair color. What else can police do? How can police gather more complete and accurate information from the young eyewitness?

ENHANCING FREE RECALL

How can free recall be enhanced to increase recall information from eyewitnesses? The options described in this section are used to elicit further event details and in some instances to increase person/perpetrator descriptors. However, as mentioned previously, these techniques are not designed specifically or exclusively for eliciting person descriptors.

Probes

One option to increase recall information from eyewitnesses is using probes. *Probes* are short, open-ended prompts that ask the witness whether he or she can remember anything else. Probes such as "What else do you remember?" or "Tell me more about what you remember" are often needed to elicit additional information. These probes, however, may not provide a substantial increase in information.

Specific Questioning

To gather more information, another option for interviewers is to ask witnesses specific questions. Roebers, Bjorklund, Schneider, and Cassel (2002) investigated how American and German children in kindergarten, Grade 2, or Grade 4, as well as adults, performed in an interview 1 week after being shown a short video of a staged theft. During the interview, participants were asked to freely recall details of the video and then answer either misleading or unbiased cued recall questions. Roebers et al. found that the three groups of children were comparable to each other, but all were significantly worse than the adult participants in free recall of appearance-related items. However, for central items (i.e., items that were critical to describing the event that had been viewed), the adults and older children (9–10-year-olds) recalled significantly more than the 7- to 8-year-olds, who in turn remembered significantly more central items than the 5- to 6-year-olds. For the unbiased cued recall questions, the percentage of correct information significantly increased for each age group as the age of the group got older. When misleading cued recall questions were asked, 5- to 6-year-olds provided more incorrect information related to central items than 7- to 8-year-olds or 9- to 10-year-olds, who were comparable to each other. Adults provided the least amount of inaccurate information when asked misleading questions. For appearance-related items, adults and the two groups of older children performed comparably, and all three of the groups performed better than the 5- to 6-year-olds. With misleading or suggestive questioning, there appears to be a decreasing trend, with adults and older children reporting fewer appearance-related inaccuracies than younger children.

In another study, Candel, Hayne, Strange, and Prevoo (2009) examined the effect of three different types of suggestions in relation to children's recognition memory for both seen and unseen objects. The study involved 7- to 11-year-olds who were asked to listen to a class presentation about China. The following day, children participated in a recognition memory task as part of the "suggestive interview," which involved them referring to information they had heard the day before. The task consisted of three types of questions: (a) questions suggesting that presented details were absent (omission errors), (b) questions suggesting that details were present when in fact they were not (commission errors), and (c) questions suggesting that details were presented differently (change errors).

One day after the suggestive interview, a new interviewer asked the children to provide her with a free recall or free narrative account of the events that took place during the presentation (i.e., "Tell me everything you can remember about the presentation and the presenter"). Finally, children would be provided with an oral recognition memory task requiring them to identify whether the items presented to them were present during the presentation. This final stage was crucial in determining whether the suggestible questions had an impact on children's memory. Half of the items presented were correct (i.e., they referred to details present in the presentation), and the other half was incorrect (i.e., they referred to information that was suggested during the suggestive interview). Candel et al. (2009) concluded that during the suggestive interview, children were more likely to conform to omission errors (e.g., "The presenter didn't tell you how long the Great Wall of China is, did she?") and change errors (e.g., "Chinese people write with letters, don't they?") rather than commission errors (e.g., "A part of the presentation was about schools in China, wasn't it?"). Results also revealed that younger children were more suggestible than older children, scoring higher on all three types of suggestibility questions (meaning that they are more likely to be influenced by the misleading questions during the suggestive interview). Younger children were also more likely to make errors related to prior suggestions during the final memory test than were the older children. Although suggestive questioning may result in more information, the information is unreliable, and this technique is not recommended with young eyewitnesses (or adult eyewitnesses).

When children are asked leading, direct questions (e.g., "Do you remember in which hand the man held the knife?" when in fact it was a gun, not a knife), they are more likely to report an inaccurate response than when they are asked nonleading, direct questions (Poole & Lindsay, 1995). It can be challenging to gather more information and to ensure that information is accurate. Leading questions are not recommended for gathering more descriptive information, whether for the event or perpetrator.

Providing Feedback

In an attempt to be encouraging and supportive, interviewers may provide feedback to the young eyewitness in hopes that it will lead to more information being recalled. The type of feedback children receive following their responses can influence their answers, however, and not necessarily in a positive way. For example, an interviewer who provides approving statements to inaccurate information (e.g., "Good, that's the right answer") or disapproving statements (e.g., "That isn't right—do you remember something different?") to accurate information can elicit further inaccurate information from child witnesses (Garven, Wood, & Malpass, 2000; Sparling, Wilder, Kondash, Boyle, & Compton, 2011).

Garven et al. (2000) looked at the impact of reinforcement and cowitness information (i.e., being told what another witness said) on children; they conducted 120 interviews of 5- to 7-year-old children after a man, Paco, visited the children's classrooms. During his visits, Paco told a story and gave the children stickers and treats. Each child was interviewed both 1 week after and 3 to 4 weeks after the classroom visit. In the first interview, children were interviewed using either (a) reinforcement alone (both positive and negative), (b) cowitness information alone (i.e., told what other children had reportedly answered to a question), (c) both reinforcement and cowitness information, and (d) no reinforcement or cowitness information (i.e., control group). Although cowitness information had little impact on children's accuracy, reinforcement was shown to have a strong influence. In fact, when children were reinforced during their first interview and made false allegations against Paco, they were likely to make these same allegations in the second interview even if no reinforcement was used.

To investigate how different behaviors by interviewers might affect the accuracy of children's responses, Sparling et al. (2011) conducted a study involving only three child participants that looked at how approving and disapproving statements influenced their accuracy. They found that the children all responded more inaccurately if positively reinforced with approving statements after they had given inaccurate information. Similarly, they all provided more inaccurate information if negatively reinforced with disapproving statements after providing accurate information. When interviewing young eyewitnesses, maintaining a neutral demeanor to what is being said may be the safest strategy to elicit accurate information.

Yes/No Questions

Using direct questions that require a yes or no response or using a forced-choice format are other options for eliciting more information following a free recall account from witnesses. However, this type of questioning can be particularly problematic for preschoolers (Peterson & Biggs, 1997). For example, Waterman, Blades, and Spencer (2004) interviewed children between the ages of 5 and 9. In this study, a woman went into children's classrooms and engaged them in a discussion about familiar topics for approximately 10 minutes. The woman showed children four photographs: two of pets and two of food items. After the woman left, researchers interviewed the children using questions that required yes or no answers (e.g., "Did the lady show you a picture of a banana?") and wh- questions (e.g., "What was the lady's name?"). Half of both types of questions had answers that were unknown to the children (e.g., "How did the lady get to school this morning?"); in these cases, the correct response should have been "I don't know." Children performed similarly across both types of questions when they were answerable. However, when questions were unanswerable, children were more likely to say, "I don't know" to wh- questions than to yes/no questions. Yes/no questions are particularly problematic for children. Melnyk, Crossman, and Scullin (2007) suggested that this may be the case because these questions rely on recognition rather than recall, thus increasing the likelihood of error.

Using recall (e.g., "Tell me everything you remember") may elicit brief responses (e.g., one or two person descriptors), but those responses are more likely to be accurate.

Using these building blocks for eliciting more information from witnesses than a broad free recall statement, several interview protocols have been developed to enhance the amount of accurate information reported by the young eyewitness. Next, I describe some of these protocols. Again, these protocols are aimed at increasing recall generally and may not be geared to increasing person information specifically.

INTERVIEW PROTOCOLS

A variety of interview protocols have been developed over the years to help young (and adult) eyewitnesses to recall witnessed details. Although the protocols aim to increase the amount of accurate information generally, some of the protocols have specific aspects directed to increasing the number of accurate person details recalled. I describe some of these protocols next.

Cognitive Interview

The cognitive interview is perhaps one of the first interviews that was designed to take into account cognitive principles, such as memory storage and retrieval, to produce a standardized interviewing protocol to be used with eyewitnesses to increase the amount of correct information witnesses could recall (Geiselman, 1984). The original cognitive interview was based on four memory-retrieval techniques:

- *reinstating the context*—thinking back to the time of the crime and remembering what was in the environment, what the emotions were, and so forth;
- *reporting everything*—saying everything that can be remembered about the event and person;
- *reversing the order*—describing the sequence of the crime from different points during the crime; and

- *changing perspectives*—considering what the crime looked like from different perspectives in the environment.[1]

This procedure was designed initially with adults in mind. In one of the first studies examining the effectiveness of the cognitive interview to increase accurate information and keep inaccurate information at a minimum, Geiselman, Fisher, MacKinnon, and Holland (1985) compared a standard police interview (that allowed police to use their own questioning style), hypnosis, and the cognitive interview.[2] Adults watched a police training film of a crime. Forty-six hours after viewing the film, experienced law enforcement professionals interviewed each participant using one of the procedures (standard, hypnosis or cognitive interview). Compared with the standard police interview and hypnosis, the cognitive interview produced the greatest amount of accurate information without an increase in inaccurate information.

The cognitive interview protocol has expanded to include the following additional components focused on social dynamics (Fisher & Geiselman, 1992):

- *rapport building*—an officer should spend time building rapport with the witness and make him or her feel comfortable and supported;
- *supportive interviewer behavior*—a witness's free recall should not be interrupted; pauses should be waited out by the officer, who should express attention to what the witness is saying;

---

[1] The changing perspective component has been challenged as producing more erroneous details, in that the witness has to imagine what might have been witnessed (Boon & Noon, 1994). It is not a component that is encouraged for use.

[2] The standard interview involved two main elements. The first component was a free recall session during which children were asked to describe what they remembered in their own words. The free recall period continued until the child had exhausted all answers (indicated by the child claiming that he or she could no longer remember anything) or until 30 seconds had elapsed with no further recall. The interviewer occasionally offered minimal prompts (e.g., "And then what happened?") or asked for clarification. The second component of the interview consisted of cued recall questions to clarify or expand on what the child previously reported throughout the free recall report. Children were asked questions about any object, people, or events they previously mentioned in their narrative (e.g., "You said that Spike found something in the water. Can you tell me more about that?"). In addition, this second stage of the interview process also involved five specific questions based on five target items (e.g., "What did Molly look at with the magnifying glass?"). The child was asked these questions regardless of whether they previously provided any information for the target item (i.e., during the free recall period), and once again, the interview concluded when the child indicated he or she could remember no more information.

- *transfer of control*—the witness, not the officer, should control the flow of the interview, since the witness, not the officer, is the expert—that is, the person who saw the crime;
- *focused retrieval*—questions should be open-ended and not leading or suggestive; after free recall, the officer should use focused memory techniques to facilitate retrieval; and
- *witness-compatible questioning*—an officer's questions should match the witness's thinking—if the witness is talking about clothing, the officer should be asking about clothing.

This enhanced cognitive interview was compared with the original and a standard (i.e., free recall followed with direct questioning) police interview (Memon & Bull, 1991). Both types of cognitive interviews produced more accurate information than the standard interview without an increase in inaccurate information.

The cognitive interview has been tested in the United Kingdom with different-age participants, including younger adults (ages 17–31), older adults (ages 60–74), and older older adults (ages 75–95; A. M. Wright & Holliday, 2007). Compared with a standard police interview, the cognitive interview increased the amount of accurate person, action, object, and surrounding details for each age group without increasing the amount of inaccurate information recalled.[3]

A meta-analysis examining 25 years of research on the cognitive interview with children 8 to 12 years old found that the cognitive interview produced a significant increase in accurate information with a small increase in errors (Memon, Meissner, & Fraser, 2010). Another meta-analysis found that children interviewed with the cognitive interview reported more accurate information than children interviewed in control conditions (Köhnken, Milne, Memon, & Bull, 1999; see also Holliday & Albon, 2004).

---

[3] Participants engaged in the standard interview were required to provide a narrative (i.e., using free recall) of what they remembered about the events that unfolded throughout the videotaped crime. Although the interviewer was instructed to not interrupt participants throughout their recall, they also were instructed to pursue any vague statements by asking for elaboration when necessary (e.g., "You mentioned that the perpetrator was nice looking. Can you describe him to me?"). As in the methodology used by Geiselman, Fisher, MacKinnon, and Holland (1985), long pauses were accompanied by a prompt from the interviewer to continue. Following the narrative period, participants were asked direct questions about previously asked questions.

The cognitive interview can be adapted and used with children (Geiselman & Padilla, 1988).

One example of a study using the cognitive interview with children was conducted by Memon, Cronin, Eaves, and Bull (1993). During a vision test at school, twenty-four 6- to 7-year-olds were videotaped. Two days later and then 6 weeks later they were interviewed about the event and the target's appearance with a cognitive interview and/or a standard interview. When the cognitive interview was used, a greater amount of information about locations of objects and people was obtained compared with the standard interview.

Although some police officers in the United States, Canada, and the United Kingdom have been trained to conduct cognitive interviews, some are reluctant to use it, stating that it requires too much time to conduct and that an appropriate environment is not always available. However, trained officers have reported that they use some of the cognitive interview components on a regular basis when interviewing witnesses (Dando, Wilcock, & Milne, 2009).

Self-Administered Interview

Somewhat similar to the cognitive interview is the relatively new interview protocol, the self-administered interview (SAI), developed by Gabbert, Hope, and Fisher (2009). The purpose of this protocol is to obtain high-quality evidence from witnesses in a timely manner with limited police resources. The SAI allows witnesses to note what they remember by using a specific set of instructions and questions. Gabbert et al. used two studies to assess their interview tool with adult witnesses. In Study 1, the SAI was compared with a free recall condition and a cognitive interview condition. Fifty-five adult participants watched a videotaped car break-in lasting 2 minutes and 40 seconds.

In the SAI condition, participants were provided a booklet containing five sections with information and instructions to help aid recall for what was witnessed:

- Section 1 emphasized the importance of following the instructions and working through the sections in a sequential manner.

- Section 2 contained information and instructions related to the context reinstatement and report everything sections of the cognitive interview. Witnesses were asked to provide as much complete and accurate information as possible without guessing.
- Section 3 related to person descriptor information. Witnesses were asked to give as much information as possible about the perpetrator's appearance (e.g., hair, complexion, build, distinguishing features).
- Section 4 asked witnesses to produce a sketch of the scene to restore critical spatial information (i.e., a general layout of the scene, positioning themselves and the others present).
- Section 5 contained questions pertaining to the event that witnesses may not have mentioned previously (e.g., time of day). Also, witnesses were asked to describe any other witnesses who may have seen what happened.

In the free recall (FR) condition, participants were given response booklets and were asked to report both event details and person descriptor details. Participants were also asked to provide as much complete and accurate information as possible without guessing.

In the cognitive interview (CI) condition, participants were administered a cognitive interview by a trained interviewer. All components of the cognitive interview (see the earlier section on the cognitive interview) were implemented except the change order and change perspective instructions.

Witnesses in the SAI and the CI conditions reported significantly more accurate details than witnesses in the FR condition. The number of accurate details reported did not differ between SAI and CI conditions. When the amount of reported information was grouped according to category (e.g., person, action, object, and setting), mean accuracy rates were highest in the CI condition for person and action categories and did not differ statistically between the SAI and FR conditions. Interestingly, the CI condition produced the highest mean accuracy rate for perpetrator descriptions.

The researchers conducted a second study to determine whether the SAI would be useful when there is a delay between the time the crime is witnessed and a report is given. Some participants used an SAI right after the witnessed event and others did not. All participants were then asked for free recall 1 week later. Participants who had completed the SAI reported more accurate information a week later than those who had not initially completed the SAI.

Although the SAI shows promise for adult witnesses, it is important to know whether it could be useful for child witnesses as well. Af Hjelmsäter, Strömwall, and Granhag (2012) investigated whether completion of an SAI immediately after a critical event enhances child eyewitness performance. Children 11 to 12 years old participated, with each child randomly allocated to one of six conditions. The children were asked to write their name on an envelope and place it in a special postbox just outside their school to enter a prize draw. They were informed that they might meet a man (a confederate) standing beside a car who might ask them something. The man asked the child to help him pick out a birthday present for a birthday party he was going to. He searched various parts of his car (e.g., back seat, front seat) until he finally found the gifts. This sequence of events would provide the children with a fair amount of both exposure time and level of detail when recalling the event. Immediately after this event, children were asked to fill out one of two SAI forms or to go home (the "no interview" form condition).

The six conditions varied in terms of the type of interview form and social influence. Two interview forms were used. The first was an SAI structured form that asked the child to include both a free recall description of the event and also to focus on the man they had met (including all his actions and what he said) as well as the location of the event. The second type of form was an SAI open form in which the child simply had to write down what happened during the event and to include as much information as possible (free recall with no cues as to what to focus on). The experiment also included a control group that did not complete any SAI form, and thus their immediate memory of the event would not be recorded. The control group's results would be compared with the descriptions provided by the children who completed the SAI forms as a test of accuracy.

The children were called in to be interviewed 2 weeks later. Before the interview, half the children were subjected to social influence by the same man they had met 2 weeks before, and the other half were not subjected to this. While waiting for the interview, the man approached the child and told him or her that he was also being interviewed and that it was important that they both say the same thing. He went over the series of events with the child, providing a correct version of the story except for four false details (i.e., he was wearing glasses). The interviewer asked the child to provide a free recall description of the events, as well as open-ended specific questions and specific questions about the four false details the man had described to the child before the interview.

Results revealed that children in the SAI structured condition reported more details (an average of 23.46) than did those who completed the SAI open form (an average of 19.88). Overall, children in both of the SAI conditions reported an average of approximately 3 details more than those children who did not complete an SAI form.

The SAI may be a promising protocol, but it is relatively new and requires further investigation with young eyewitnesses of various ages to determine its efficacy. Practical elements of the SAI have to be considered as well, such as cost of interviewer training, amount of time required to conduct the SAI, and whether the SAI may be more or less useful with eyewitnesses of various ages. Specific issues for young eyewitnesses include at what age the steps and instructions exceed a child's ability to comprehend what is required and the amount of time a young child can be interviewed before fatigue sets in.

Step-Wise Interview

The step-wise interview, developed by Yuille, Hunter, Joffe, and Zaparniuk (1993), had two goals: (a) to maximize the amount of information recalled and (b) to minimize contamination of this information by interviewer influence. This interview process involves the following nine steps:

1. *Building rapport.* The interviewer should engage the child in conversation about neutral events until the child is comfortable with the

interviewer. The interviewer should make informal observations of the child regarding cognitive and social skills, language, and behavior during this time.

2. *Requesting recall of two specific events.* The child is asked to describe two neutral events from the past, such as a birthday party or class field trip. This gives a baseline of how much information the child will typically provide, extends rapport building, and helps model the interview style for the child.

3. *Telling the truth.* The interviewer establishes that the child knows he or she has to tell the truth by asking increasingly specific questions related to what it means to tell the truth or to lie. The purpose of this is to establish interview integrity from the beginning.

4. *Introducing the topic of concern.* First, the child is asked in an open-ended way whether he or she is aware of the purpose of the interview. The interviewer cannot name the suspect or allegations under any circumstances. If the child is not forthcoming, he or she is asked to draw an outline of a man or woman and name the parts of the body and describe their purpose. After this, the child is asked to draw an outline of the other sex and name the parts of the body.

5. *Using free narrative.* Children are then asked to freely report the event(s) that occurred related to the topic of concern. For multiple events, the child can be asked to give a general description of what happened during the events and then give details about specific events. It is helpful for the interviewer to label the events once the child has described them (e.g., the playground event).

6. *Asking general questions.* To gain more information, the interviewer can then ask the child general questions but only using information the child has provided and only involving terms the child has used. If the child is hesitant to talk about certain events, the interviewer can ask him or her to provide a nonverbal signal when he or she is uncomfortable talking about something, rather than not remembering it.

7. *Asking specific questions (when necessary).* In a best-case scenario, specific questioning will not be needed because all pertinent information would have already been obtained. However, if clarification is needed,

specific questions are asked using the general technique of the cognitive interview described previously in this chapter. Multiple-choice questions should be avoided unless necessary; when necessary, multiple-choice questions should have three or more response options and should be re-presented with the options in a different order later in the interview to confirm that the choice was due to accuracy rather than response bias. Inconsistencies in the child's description can be gently investigated during this time as well. At the end of this step, the child should be asked to freely recall the event(s) again.

8. *Using interview aids (when necessary).* Drawings, dolls without genitals, and anatomically correct dolls may be used in a step-wise method when required. When the suggestibility of a child is of concern, the interviewer can test this with questions unrelated to the purpose of the interview, such as "You came here by taxi, didn't you?" (Yuille et al., 1993, p. 109). If a child is deemed susceptible, the interview results will have to be examined carefully for contamination.

9. *Concluding the interview.* If another adult was present during the interview in the role of a recorder, the interviewer will ask the recorder for any questions he or she has.[4] After the recorder asks the child these questions, the child is thanked and informed about what will happen next. The child can then ask questions of the interviewer.

The step-wise interview follows the general principles of good interviewing with child eyewitnesses. It is an interview protocol used in some jurisdictions in Canada. Some interviewers use portions or some steps with young eyewitnesses.

The step-wise interview protocol (SWI) has recently undergone significant changes to make the protocol more useful with younger children and to more clearly differentiate between each questioning stage (Lindberg, Chapman, Samsock, Thomas, & Lindberg, 2003). Specifically, the revised protocol provides a detailed three-step procedure for the disclosure of sexual abuse. First, an uninterrupted free narrative account of the events is

---

[4] Although ideally only one adult will be present, it is often required that two are, such as when a police officer and social worker are both required to witness the interview. In such situations, one acts as the interviewer and the other sits quietly, observing and recording the interview information.

elicited, followed by a second step, in which the child is to answer a series of specific, nonleading, open-ended questions prompting for the who, what, where, and when information associated with the event. The third step is a specific questioning phase during which the interviewer asks the child for further clarification of or elaboration on any previously mentioned narratives or answers. However, in the revised version of the SWI, the last step is to be used only in cases where the child has previously provided insufficient detail. A clarification step was also introduced in the revised SWI in which the interviewer would be able to ask questions to clarify previous inconsistencies or contradictions.

In addition, there have been broader modifications made to the original SWI according to developmental guidelines (Bottoms, Najdowski, & Goodman, 2009). For example, it has been advised that nonsuggestive means be used in the rapport building stage and that adequate time be provided for the child to practice telling about events and responding to open-ended questions as well as to practice using evidence-based memory. There have been suggestions made to promote establishing a set of ground rules for the duration of the interview. That is, children should be instructed to tell only the truth and to say "I don't know" or "I don't remember" rather than fabricating a statement. In addition, children should be reminded that they are free to ask for clarification of any question rather than interpreting the question in a different way. For specific questions, the use of "Wh" questions should be used as follow-ups to elicit more details about a previously disclosed statement. Interviewers should also avoid double negatives (e.g., "Didn't he hurt you?"), suppositional questions (e.g., "When he hurt you, was he happy or mad?"), and multiple-choice questions (although these questions are deemed appropriate if asking for clarification after an open-ended question).

Lindberg et al. (2003) examined three separate interview techniques, including the SWI, a doll play interview developed by Action for Child Protection, and the modified structured interview. The purpose of the study was to explore which interview technique was most effective against coached or falsified information. The doll play interview, typically used by child protective services, was intended to be accommodative and sensitive to the child's emotions. The interviewer pays close attention to any fears and anxieties displayed by the child and asks prompting questions (e.g., "And what happened next?") if the interviewer has found the child's response to be surprising. The interviewers were instructed on how to use five different types of questions:

- General questions such as "How are you?" or "Tell me more about that." These questions were labeled as most reliable.
- Focused questions such as "How are you getting along with your father?"
- Multiple-choice questions such as "Did he hit you with his hand or a stick?"
- Yes or no questions such as "Did he tell you not to tell?"
- Leading questions such as "He made you sleep outside, didn't he?" These questions were labeled as least reliable.

In the final component of the doll play interview, the child was asked to portray what happened using a series of plastic dolls.

The SWI procedure was kept consistent with the procedure outlined by Yuille et al. (1993). Using the modified structured interview, interviewers would begin the session with a free narrative of the events that occurred, followed by specific questions about five distinct categories accompanied by relevant follow-up questions for each. The categories focused on asking questions to assist the child in recalling more who, what, when, and where details of the incident:

- Fearful questions, such as "When you watched the movie, who would you be most afraid of?"
- "Who was present?" type questions, such as "Who was in the room when it happened?"
- "How" questions, such as "Did they hold, touch, or hit anything?"
- "Where" questions, such as "Please tell me something about the room, playground, house, and so forth."
- Questions aimed at detecting coached information, such as "Did anyone ask you to tell me anything about what you saw?"

Results suggested that the modified structured interview was superior at detecting coached information. It resulted in a six-fold increase in accuracy for where information compared with the doll play interview and SWI. In addition, children interviewed using the SWI and modified structure interview provided more recall in terms of number of objects remembered during the free narrative sessions.

Hardy and Van Leeuwen (2004) devised a slightly modified version of the SWI protocol to examine the effects of the interview procedure on young (3–5.5 years old) versus older children (5.5–8 years old). The experimental protocol (i.e., the modified procedure) altered probes in the rapport building, topic introduction, and specific questioning stages of the SWI. Specifically, during rapport building, children were asked to focus on a past event or favorite game or activity, whereas in the original SWI they were simply asked to provide a free narrative of a neutral past event. Instead of orienting the child to a target event during the topic introduction, the experimental protocol made specific reference to the target event. Finally, specific questions throughout the experimental protocol asked who, where, what, and when, with follow-up questions for the purpose of clarification, whereas the original SWI focused on asking questions by cycling between open-ended and specific questions as new topics were brought up. Results suggested that younger children reported less information and were less accurate and more prone to suggestion than older children. Young children were least accurate when asked direct questions and asked to recall a specific past event during the rapport-building phase.

Narrative Elaboration

The narrative elaboration procedure was developed by Saywitz and Snyder (1996) to aid children's recall by helping them organize their story into relevant categories: participants, settings, actions, conversation or affective states, and consequences. A line drawing is available for each category. These visual cues help children remember to report all they can. Children practice telling stories with each card before being questioned about the critical event. They are then asked for a free narrative about the critical event and person—for example, "What did he look like?" Last, children are presented with each card and asked, "Does this card remind you to tell something else?"

To test the narrative elaboration procedure, children in Grades 1 and 2 and children in Grades 4, 5, and 6 witnessed a staged event (Saywitz & Snyder, 1996). The children were then interviewed using either the narrative elaboration procedure (involving training in the use of reminder cue cards), exposure to the cue cards without training, or a standard interview without training or cue cards.[5] Children interviewed with the narrative elaboration procedures reported more accurate information but not more inaccurate information for the staged event compared with just the cue cards being presented without training or the standard interview. Also, children did not fabricate more information with the narrative elaboration procedure.

Given the positive effects of the narrative elaboration procedure, D. Brown and Pipe (2003) considered whether they could further improve the procedure if mental reinstatement was included. Six- to 9-year-olds were interviewed using narrative elaboration training or narrative elaboration training with mental reinstatement. There was also a control condition without training for narrative elaboration. Children were read a fictional story, after which they were given a recollection task for which they were to recall as much as they could, being reminded that completeness and accuracy was important. The children then completed a categorization task in which they were shown a series of cards depicting common objects (e.g., clothing, furniture) and were asked to sort the objects that belong together. Next, before being dismissed, each child was asked to tell the interviewer everything he or she could remember about his or her morning commute to school. The following day after training, each child was asked to recall the story from the day before. Children trained with narrative elaboration reported twice as much information and were

---

[5] The standard interview consisted of three tasks. The first was a free recall period in which the child was instructed to provide a narrative of everything he or she could remember about what he or she witnessed. The next task involved cued recall; each child was shown a visual cue (i.e., a cue card) for the purpose of elaborating on his or her narrative. The third and final task involved probed recall; children were asked multiple short-answer questions about the events they witnessed (e.g., "Who was there? What did they look like? What was his name?").

more accurate compared with the control group. Mental reinstatement did not increase accuracy. Moreover, research has found that simply asking children to report what they saw and heard or to talk about information across categories was sufficient to produce increases in the amount of information recalled (Quas, Schaaf, Alexander, & Goodman, 2000). In a study examining the techniques used by forensic interviewers in 137 cases of sexual abuse, narrative elaboration was used infrequently, in only about 12% of the cases (Faller, Grabarek, Nelson-Gardell, & Williams, 2011). The narrative elaboration protocol does have a cue for person and may be useful in increasing the amount and accuracy of person details.

National Institute of Child Health and Human Development Interview Protocol

After having examined a number of interviewing protocols for use with children, Michael Lamb and his colleagues at the National Institute of Child Health and Human Development (NICHD) developed an interviewing procedure that relies on open-ended questioning with two types of prompts available to interviewers (Sternberg, Lamb, Esplin, Orbach, & Hershkowitz, 2002). Interviewers can use time prompts to help the child fill in details and a timeline. For example, the interviewer may ask, "What happened next?" Also, interviewers can use cue question prompts incorporating details the child previously reported on which he or she is asked to elaborate. For example, the interviewer may say, "You said the teacher took off his belt. Tell me more about that." This protocol also provides direction on how to start the interview and how to introduce the topic of abuse. For example, children are initially engaged in describing neutral events (e.g., the child's guitar lessons) in a nonleading manner. The topic of abuse may be introduced by asking the child why he or she has come to talk to you. A number of studies have been conducted investigating the NICHD protocol with positive results (Lamb, Hershkowitz, Orbach, & Esplin, 2008). It should be noted that this protocol is more focused on recalling event details of abuse rather than specifically trying to garner more accurate information about person descriptors.

Orbach et al. (2000) investigated the effectiveness of the interviews conforming to the NICHD structured protocol in comparison with interviews that did not follow the protocol. They did this by looking at 55 interviews of children conducted following the protocol and 50 nonprotocol interviews that had been administered by the same interviewers. All interviewed children were between the ages of 4 and 13. Orbach et al. (2000) found that older children consistently provided more information than younger children. They also found that the interviewing practices in the protocol interviews were much more desirable because these interviews included more open-ended questions and fewer suggestive, directive, or closed-ended questions. Research has shown that open-ended questioning results in more accurate information being provided than questioning that engages recognition rather than recall (e.g., Dent & Stephenson, 1979). Orbach et al. (2000) suggested that although no more information was provided using the NICHD structured interviews, this information was likely more accurate than that provided using the other interviews.

Sternberg, Lamb, Orbach, Esplin, and Mitchell (2001) also compared interviews conducted using the NICHD structured interview protocol with interviews using standard procedures. The children were between the ages of 4 and 12, and children in each group were matched on age, relationship to offender, and the seriousness of the crime. Like Orbach et al. (2000), Sternberg et al. found that the NICHD protocol resulted in more open-ended prompting by interviewers and less suggestive or closed-ended questioning. When open-ended prompts were used, there were no age differences in the amount of information provided. Furthermore, 89% of the children interviewed with the NICHD structured protocol made allegations in open-ended questioning, compared with only 36% of the children in the standard interview condition.

One aspect of the NICHD protocol that can occur and appears problematic for children 4 to 9 years is a multipart prompt where interviewers ask two prompts together—for example, "Tell me everything about how he caught you? When did it happen?" The use of multipart prompts is not recommended for collecting as much information as possible. Multipart prompts also can be problematic for adults (Bassili & Scott, 1996).

SPECIFIC TECHNIQUES FOR INCREASING DETAILS

Some specific techniques have been investigated to aid in increasing the number and accuracy of details reported by young eyewitnesses. I describe some of these techniques next.

Using a Reference

Kask, Bull, Heinla, and Davies (2007) investigated the use of a person as a "standard" to aid children 6 to 9 years old in describing a different person, the confederate, they had seen 1 hour previously for approximately 1 minute. All participants were initially asked to freely recall what the confederate looked like before being asked any specific questions. For half the participants, the interviewer acted as a standard, asking them questions in relation to themselves (e.g., "My hair is this long. How long was his hair?"; p. 79). The other half of the group was asked the same type of questions with no standard. Kask et al. found no significant difference in the accuracy of children's descriptions of the confederate when using or not using a standard. They did find, however, that when the interviewer/standard was female, it helped the boys more than it did the girls.

Drawing

Katz and Hershkowitz (2012) were interested in whether allowing children to draw about the event during an interview would affect how much information they provided. In their study, 125 participants between the ages of 4 and 14 were interviewed; 69 of the participants were asked to engage in drawing during the first interview, whereas the rest were not. All participants were then interviewed again. In both conditions, children provided significantly more information about the central details of the event than about peripheral details. The children also remembered more details that described locations and actions rather than people. The children in the drawing group remembered a greater proportion of information regarding people, locations, and actions than did the nondrawers. Thus, drawing may be a helpful tool with person descriptions. However, more research is needed to establish the parameters of when and how this might be useful.

Closing Your Eyes

Mastroberardino, Natali, and Candel (2012) studied whether closing one's eyes while recounting an event has any effect on the number of details that are reported. Closing one's eyes reduces external stimulation, consequently allocating more resources to the mental visual memory trace. Six- and 11-year-olds watched a 7-minute clip of a scene from *Jurassic Park* (none of the children had seen the movie previously) in which a man is in a car with children when a tyrannosaurus attacks. Participants in both the eyes open and eyes closed conditions were asked to provide a free recall account of what had happened in the scene they had just watched. Next, the children were asked a series of cue recall questions eliciting more specific details (using information previously provided by the children during the free recall phase), such as the number of people involved in the scene. Participants in both conditions (eyes open vs. eyes closed) were given the same instructions, except that children in the eyes closed condition were asked to keep their eyes closed during the questioning period.

Findings revealed that younger children (i.e., 6-year-olds) fabricated more than older children (i.e., 11-year-olds). Results also revealed that both younger and older children in the eyes closed, free recall condition reported more correct details (13.39 and 40.16 details, respectively) than younger and older children in the eyes open condition (13.16 and 36.44 details, respectively). The results were similar for cued recall. Children in the eyes closed condition made significantly fewer errors when reporting the details of the scene than did children in the eyes open condition. Allowing young eyewitnesses to close their eyes when recalling may be helpful, but again, more research is needed.

CONCLUSION

The keys to the successful use of protocols when interviewing the young eyewitness include using free recall, limiting directive questioning, and avoiding suggestive or misleading questions. No one protocol has been adopted across all jurisdictions; rather, certain protocols are more popular in some areas, and various elements are common across a number of protocols. Some emphasis should be placed on techniques that can elicit person information or descriptors that can aid police in their investigations, particularly when perpetrators are unknown to the eyewitnesses. Although good interviewing practices are a starting point, there may be specific techniques that help the young eyewitness to provide these critical details. Greater attention should be focused on helping young eyewitnesses provide accurate person descriptors.

4

Effects of Lineup Construction and Procedures

As in the cases presented in Chapter 1 and in many others, once police have a suspect, the eyewitness will be asked to identify the perpetrator. A common method used to prove the identity of the perpetrator is to conduct a lineup identification, in which a witness views individuals, including a suspect, and determines whether one of the individuals presented is the perpetrator. Thus, the eyewitness is asked to identify the perpetrator (rather than the "suspect") when shown a lineup.

Some information about the identity of the perpetrator is gained from the description provided by the eyewitness, but as discussed in Chapter 2, descriptions tend to be brief and can apply to many, although verbal descriptions do provide some information about the perpetrator. When an eyewitness identifies a suspect as the perpetrator from a lineup, it is more likely that the suspect is the perpetrator (Wells, 1993). In contrast, if a suspect is not identified, the likelihood that the suspect is the perpetrator

http://dx.doi.org/10.1037/14956-005
The Young Eyewitness: How Well Do Children and Adolescents Describe and Identify Perpetrators?
by J. Pozzulo

is decreased (Wells & Lindsay, 1980). For a lineup to be useful, lineup construction is critical. A number of issues have to be addressed when conducting a lineup identification procedure. A variety of procedures have been developed and tested. In this chapter, I describe lineup construction as well as lineup procedures and the efficacy of those procedures.

LINEUP CONSTRUCTION

Single-Suspect Versus Multiple-Suspect Model

When constructing a lineup, two models of lineup construction are possible: (a) multiple suspect and (b) single suspect (Wells & Turtle, 1986). Consider the situation in which a crime has occurred and the police have a few suspects who may be guilty, but they cannot narrow it down any further. The *multiple-suspect model* includes all the suspects for the same crime in one lineup. The difficulty with this model is that no matter whom the witness selects, it is considered a positive identification and that suspect will be pursued, whether or not he or she is the perpetrator. This type of lineup model does not allow for any protection against a false identification. In Chapter 1, I discussed the three decisions possible with a lineup, including a *foil* identification. If a foil (i.e., a lineup member who is known to be innocent) is identified as the perpetrator, police know that the witness has made a mistake. A foil identification allows police to differentiate witnesses who may have a poor memory of the perpetrator. Without foils in a lineup, police have no way of assessing a witness's memory for the perpetrator. Foils provide protection for a suspect. Without foils, any identification is an identification of a suspect.

A *single-suspect model* includes one suspect and a set of foils. The number of foils can vary by jurisdiction, but typically the range is three to 11 foils (and one suspect). Should police have multiple suspects, each suspect should be placed in his or her own lineup with a set of foils for each, using different foils for each suspect.

Foils

Police can use two types of strategies to decide on the physical appearance of the lineup foils. A *similarity-to-suspect* strategy matches lineup members to the suspect's appearance. For example, if the suspect has brown hair, blue eyes, and a mustache, then each lineup member would have these characteristics. A difficulty with this strategy, however, is that there are many physical features that could be matched, such as width of eyebrows, length of nose, thickness of lips, and so on. If taken to the extreme, this strategy would produce a lineup of people who would look exactly like the suspect, making it virtually impossible to identify the perpetrator even if the witness has a good memory of the perpetrator. In contrast, a *match-to-description* strategy sets limits on the number of features that have to be matched. With this strategy, foils are matched only on the items the witness provided in his or her description. For example, if a witness stated that the criminal had brown hair, blue eyes, a round face, and was clean-shaven, those would be the features on which each lineup member is matched.

Fitzgerald, Whiting, Therrien, and Price (2014) examined the effect of foil similarity on children's identifications by comparing the identification accuracy of both children and adults using either a higher similarity (to the suspect) lineup or a lower similarity lineup. They found that children were less likely to make a correct identification with a higher similarity than a lower similarity *target-present* (i.e., suspect is guilty) lineup; there was no effect on the rate of correct identifications by adults. However, this correct identification improvement for children with the lower similarity lineup was also associated with an increased rate of innocent suspect identifications in *target-absent* (i.e., suspect is innocent) lineups. This indicates that the cost–benefit relationship of increased correct identifications versus increased mistaken identifications should be weighed carefully when choosing how closely foils resemble the suspect in lineups presented to child eyewitnesses.

Lindsay, Martin, and Webber (1994) noted that some general characteristics that might not be mentioned would have to be included to produce a fair lineup. A *fair lineup* is one in which the suspect does not stand out from the other lineup members. For example, if skin color was not mentioned, a lineup constructed with one white face (the suspect) and five black faces would be unfair or biased. Some characteristics, such as sex, race, and age, are known as default values and should be matched even if not mentioned in the witness's description.

To avoid a biased lineup, Luus and Wells (1991; Wells, Rydell, & Seelau, 1993) further suggested that if a feature provided in the witness's description does not match the suspect's appearance, the foils should match the suspect's appearance on that feature. For example, if the perpetrator is described as having red hair but the suspect has blond hair, the foils should have blond hair.

Live Versus "Photographic" Versus Video Lineups

Photo array is the term used for photographic lineups. In the United States and Canada, police typically now use a set of photographs rather than live persons to assemble a lineup. This was also the case decades ago (Wells & Turtle, 1986). However, in the United Kingdom, police are advised to use video lineups (Police and Criminal Evidence Act [PACE] Code D 2011, Home Office and The Rt Hon Nick Herbert). Live lineups are permitted in the United Kingdom under some circumstances, but photo lineups are typically not (PACE Code D, 2011). Thus, some form of photo technology (i.e., photographs or video display) is the common format for lineups.

Photo technology may be more common than live lineups for the following reasons:

- They are less time consuming to construct. The police can choose foils from their mug shot database (i.e., pictures of people who have been charged with crimes in the past) rather than find live persons.
- They are portable. The police are able to bring the photo array to the witness rather than have the witness go to the police department, making it possibly less stressful and more convenient for the witness to view the lineup at a different location than the police station.
- A suspect has no legal obligation to participate in a lineup without a court order before his or her arrest. Therefore, before arrest, it is easier

to obtain a photograph of the suspect for identification purposes (or one may already be on file) than to have the suspect agree to participate in a live lineup. Once an arrest has taken place, a suspect has the right to counsel before participating in either a photo or video lineup (*Kirby v. Illinois*, 1972; *R v. Sinclair*, 2010).

- Because photos are static, the police need not worry that the suspect's behavior may draw attention to him- or herself, thereby invalidating the photo array.
- A witness may be less anxious examining a photo array than a live lineup.

Other advantages of video lineups include the ability to enlarge faces or focus on particular features. Lineup members can be shown walking, turning, and talking. For example, Humphries, Holliday, and Flowe (2012) examined identification abilities of younger children (M_{age} = 5.8), older children (M_{age} = 9.8), and adults (M_{age} = 20) across simultaneous, sequential, and elimination video lineups (more about these lineups a bit later on). Participants were shown a videotaped crime depicting a theft of a purse and were then presented with either a target-present or target-absent video lineup. Video lineups included a moving picture of each lineup member. Image clips were color head-and-shoulder shots. Each lineup member started in a full frontal pose, then turned to a left profile pose, a right profile pose, and a final full frontal pose. Each lineup member was viewed for approximately 15 seconds. Adults were more likely to correctly identify the target in the sequential lineup (at a rate of .83) than were younger (at a rate of .30) and older children (at a rate of .47). No age-related differences were found for correct identification rates between the simultaneous and elimination lineups. When presented with target-absent lineups, adults were significantly more likely to make a correct rejection than were younger and older children. There was a trend for higher correct rejection rates for adults in the elimination lineup (.80) compared with the simultaneous video lineup (.60). No other age-related differences were examined across lineup type.

Beresford and Blades (2006) conducted another study examining both photo and video lineups. Participants included younger children (ages 6–7) and older children (ages 9–10). The participants were exposed to a property theft and subsequently asked to identify the thief from a lineup. Beresford and Blades manipulated the type of lineup procedure (simultaneous or elimination; lineup procedures will be described later), type of lineup media (video or photo), and type of lineup instructions (standard vs. cautioning, where cautioning stressed the importance of not making a false identification) for each of the two separate age groups. Age had no significant influence on any of the results. For all target-present conditions, correct identification rates were similar when all results were included in the analyses. For target-absent photo lineups, the elimination lineup procedure was associated with significantly more correct rejections than the simultaneous lineup procedure, with no impact of type of lineup instruction when all results were included. For target-absent video line-ups, cautioning instructions were associated with a higher rate of correct rejections, but there was no impact of type of lineup procedure.

Beresford and Blades (2006) ran additional analyses that they consid-ered consequential to the justice system; they ignored foil identifications in target-present conditions as well as target-absent conditions. Again, age was not found to predict accuracy in any of the conditions. They found that, using these criteria, the odds of a correct identification versus an incor-rect rejection was significantly lower for the elimination lineup compared with the simultaneous lineup procedure for the video lineup. No differences between the two lineup procedures were found in target-present conditions when the lineup media was photographic. No differences in accuracy were found between the elimination lineup procedure and simultaneous lineup procedure for target-absent lineups. However, cautioning instruc-tions were associated with a higher likelihood of a correct rejection for all lineup procedures.

Number of Lineup Members Shown

How many lineup members are shown to an eyewitness varies by jurisdic-tion. Lineups in some parts of the United States can be four person or six person. For example, West Virginia requires a minimum of five persons in the lineup (i.e., at least four fillers/foils and the target). Similarly, the state of Washington requires a minimum of five persons, although six is preferred. New York requires at least six persons in the lineup (i.e., at least five fillers/foils and the suspect).

In a study investigating whether lineup size matters, Pozzulo, Dempsey, and Wells (2010) examined young eyewitnesses' identification abilities as a function of lineup size. Children ages 8 to 13 years (M_{age} = 10.37 years) were shown a videotaped, nonviolent crime depicting a theft from a school locker and were then presented with either a 6- or 12-person elimination lineup. Participants were partitioned into two age groups, younger (8–10 years old) and older (11–13 years old), to examine any possible age differences. The overall correct identification rates did not differ statistically between the younger children (.35) and older children (.20). It should be noted that cell sizes were small, and a 15% difference when applied to the real world is quite dramatic (i.e., 15% of perpetrators would not be identified). When presented with a target-absent lineup, younger children and older children produced similar correct rejection rates (.50 vs. .57, respectively). The two groups were then combined to examine overall accuracy. When presented with a target-present lineup, children produced nonsignificantly different rates of correct identification for both the six-person (.25) and 12-person lineup (.36). Also, when presented with a target-absent lineup, nonsignificantly different correct rejections rates were observed for both the six-person (.48) and 12-person lineup (.59). These results suggest that for eyewitnesses between 8 to 13 years old, a lineup size of six to 12 persons might not hinder children's performance. However, this conclusion should be considered tentative, given the size of the sample and the fact that the data are derived from just this is one study. Further work should explore whether age interacts with lineup size (and whether lineup medium and procedure matter).

LINEUP PROCEDURES

Lineups can be presented to the eyewitness in different formats and/or with different procedures. No one procedure is consistent across all jurisdictions. It is not uncommon for neighboring cities and towns to use different procedures when administering lineups. Next, I describe the lineup procedures that have been investigated empirically.

Simultaneous Lineup

Perhaps the most common lineup procedure used in various parts of the world, the *simultaneous lineup* (Wells, 1993), presents all lineup members at one time to the witness. This procedure is the one shown in television shows and movies, with the witness behind a one-way mirror with the police officer and the lineup members on the other side of the mirror to be viewed by the witness. The simultaneous lineup also can be administered using photographs. The police display all the lineup members in photographs on a table in front of the witness. Wells (1993) suggested that the simultaneous lineup procedure encourages the witness to make a relative judgment, whereby lineup members are compared with each other and the person who looks most like the perpetrator is identified. The simultaneous lineup was not designed for a witness of a particular age; it has been used widely with young children, adults, and the elderly. The young eyewitness Kathy Sigman, described in Chapter 1, was shown a simultaneous lineup.

Marin, Holmes, Guth, and Kovac (1979) conducted one of the first studies examining children's identification rates with the simultaneous lineup procedure using an eyewitness. Several age groups were compared, including kindergarteners and first graders, third and fourth graders, seventh and eighth graders, and undergraduate students. The experimenter and an assistant greeted participants when they entered the testing room and told them to take a seat. After a few minutes, a confederate entered the room, interrupted the "testing" session, and explained to the experimenter that he had booked the room and needed it right away. The confederate then stated that someone would hear about the mishap, and he left the room. After a delay of 10 or 30 minutes, participants were asked to identify the confederate from a set of six photographs. Only a target-present lineup was used, so the confederate's photo was among the photos presented. Correct identification rates did not differ across age groups. Even the youngest participants identified the confederate at a rate comparable to adults.

J. F. Parker, Haverfield, and Baker-Thomas (1986) attempted to replicate the finding of Marin et al. (1979) using two different age targets: children (M_{age} = 9 years) and adults (M_{age} = 24 years). The identification abilities of middle-age children (M_{age} = 8 years) were compared with those of undergraduate students (M_{age} = 24 years). A slide sequence was used to expose participants to the targets. Participants saw one of the two targets in the sequence that depicted a theft of a radio and blanket in an outdoor picnic area and then were shown a six-person, target-present, simultaneous photographic lineup. After a series of questions concerning the crime, participants were shown a second lineup with the same photos but in different positions. As in the Marin et al. (1979) study, correct identification rates did not differ between children and adults for either of the targets. When examining the reliability of the identification, children were more likely to change their lineup choice between the first and second identification tasks.

To follow up this work, J. F. Parker and Carranza (1989) conducted a study that included target-present and target-absent lineups. Middle-age children (M = 9 years) and adults (M = 21 years) were shown a slide sequence that included either a child target or an adult target. As in the J. F. Parker and colleagues (1986) study, participants were presented with a slide sequence that depicted the theft of a radio and blanket in an outdoor picnic area. Six-person photographic lineups were created for each target. After the slide sequence, participants were presented with either a target-present or target-absent lineup. After a series of questions, participants were presented with a second lineup that included the same target and fillers/foils but in a different order. The rate of correct identification was nonsignificantly different across both age groups, as was the rate of correct rejection.

Pozzulo and Dempsey (2006) examined the identification abilities of children (M_{age} = 10.56 years) and adults (M_{age} = 20.30 years) when presented with a target-absent simultaneous lineup. Participants were shown a video of a confederate (named Mike) discussing how to stay safe. After roughly a 20-minute delay, participants completed the identification task. Half the participants were given neutral instructions (i.e., indicating that Mike may or may not be present), whereas the other half were given biased instructions (i.e., placing a check in the box that has the same number as Mike's picture). When given the neutral instructions, children had significantly lower correct rejection rates (.54) than did adults (.87); similar results were found when biased instructions were given (.11 for children vs. .44 for adults). A second study that used the same design with a different event and target produced similar results. Children had lower correct rejection rates in both the neutral and biased conditions than did adults.

Pozzulo, Dempsey, Crescini, and Lemieux (2009, Study 2) further examined identification abilities of children (M_{age} = 10.35 years) and adults (M_{age} = 20.92 years) when presented with a simultaneous lineup. Participants were shown a videotaped staged theft of a woman's purse. After roughly 20 minutes, participants were presented with either a target-present or target-absent lineup. Correct identification rates were non-significantly different for children (.50) and adults (.67); however, as in previous research, children's correct rejection rates were significantly lower (.17) than were adults' (.50) when presented with a target-absent lineup.

Over the past 30 years, a number of studies have examined the young eyewitness's abilities with a simultaneous lineup. The most predominant finding was that the rate of correct rejection is lower for younger-young eyewitnesses compared with older-young eyewitnesses and adults and for older-young eyewitnesses compared with adults. In a meta-analysis (Pozzulo & Lindsay, 1998) examining correct identification rates and correct rejection rates across four different age groups (M_{age} = 4 years; M_{age} = 5–6 years; M_{age} = 9–10 years; and M_{age} = 12–13 years) compared with adults, children of all ages produced a lower rate of correct rejection when using a simultaneous lineup. There was some stability in correct identification between children and adults; however, a lower rate of correct identification has been found between children and adults using a simultaneous lineup procedure (Fitzgerald & Price, 2015). Perhaps different lineup procedures can improve the young eyewitness's identification accuracy.

Sequential Lineup

An alternative lineup procedure is the *sequential lineup*. This procedure was developed in the mid-1980s with the objective of combating the use of a relative judgment strategy and relying more on an absolute strategy in which the witness compares each lineup member to his or her memory of the perpetrator (Lindsay & Wells, 1985). Using this strategy, lineup members are presented serially to the witness. The witness must decide whether the lineup member is the perpetrator before seeing the next lineup member (Lindsay & Wells, 1985). The witness cannot ask to see previously presented photos, and the witness is unaware of the number of photos to be shown. Wells (1993) suggested that the sequential procedure reduces the likelihood that witnesses can make a relative judgment because they are not viewing more than one photo at a time. Instead, witnesses may be more likely to make an absolute judgment, whereby each lineup member is compared with the witness's memory of the perpetrator and the witness decides whether it is the perpetrator.

Lindsay and Wells (1985) compared the identification accuracy rate of the simultaneous and sequential lineup procedures using adult participants. University students witnessed a videotaped theft and were asked to identify the perpetrator from six photographs. Half the students saw a target-present lineup, and the other half of students saw a target-absent lineup. Across target-present and target-absent conditions, the lineups were either presented using a simultaneous procedure or a sequential procedure.

Correct identification rates (in target-present lineups) did not differ across lineup procedures. However, correct rejection rates were significantly different across lineup procedures. Only 42% of the participants made a correct rejection with a simultaneous lineup, whereas 65% of the participants made a correct rejection with a sequential lineup. In other words, if the perpetrator was not included in the lineup, adult witnesses were more likely to correctly indicate that he or she was not present if they were shown a sequential lineup, compared with when they were shown simultaneous lineup. The higher correct rejection rate with the sequential procedure compared with the simultaneous procedure has been replicated numerous times (Steblay, Dysart, Fulero, & Lindsay, 2001). Across several studies (with adult participant–witnesses), however, correct identifications have been shown to decrease with the sequential lineup compared with the simultaneous lineup (Lindsay, Mansour, Beaudry, Leach,

& Bertrand, 2009). The sequential lineup is the procedure used in some U.S. states (e.g., New Jersey), in parts of Canada, and the United Kingdom. Recent research, however, has called into question the "sequential superiority effect" over the simultaneous procedure (McQuiston-Surrett, Malpass, & Tredoux, 2006). The researchers suggested that when certain methodological factors are considered, the simultaneous procedure yields similar correct rejection rates as the sequential procedure, without a drop in correct identifications. The debate between the simultaneous and sequential lineup procedures for adult eyewitnesses is ongoing (e.g., Gronlund, Carlson, Dailey, & Goodsell, 2009; Gronlund et al., 2012; Gronlund, Wixted, & Mickes, 2014; Mecklenburg, Bailey, & Larson, 2008; Mickes, Flowe, & Wixted, 2012; Wells, Steblay, & Dysart, 2015).

How does the young eyewitness do with the sequential procedure? A number of studies have compared simultaneous and sequential lineup procedures with young eyewitnesses. For example, J. F. Parker and Ryan (1993) had 8- to 11-year-olds ($M = 9$ years) and university students ($M = 24$ years; range = 18–47 years) viewed a slide sequence of a picnic scene with a male entering at the 11th slide and stealing a radio. Participants were shown either a simultaneous or a sequential lineup. Some participants were given practice trials of the lineup procedure using the female experimenter as the target. The experimenter provided feedback on these practice trials. The other participants rank ordered photos for the equivalent amount of time as the practice trials. All participants were then shown a target-present or target-absent lineup using a simultaneous or sequential lineup procedure. The rate of correct identification did not differ significantly as a function of age or lineup procedure. In terms of correct rejections, however, children had a lower correct rejection rate than did adults, regardless of lineup procedure. Sequential presentation did not increase children's correct rejection rate compared with simultaneous presentation. Moreover, practice was not consistently beneficial. The increase in correct rejections for sequential presentation over the simultaneous lineup found in some studies with adult participants did not occur with child participants.

In another attempt to examine whether practice with sequential lineups would help young eyewitnesses, J. F. Parker and Myers (2001) had middle-age children between 8 and 10 years ($M = 9$ years) examine a 15-slide sequence of a picnic, with a male entering at the 11th slide and stealing a radio (as in J. F. Parker & Ryan, 1993). Half the children were given two practice sequential lineups with some combination of target-present and target-absent and were given feedback on their accuracy. The remaining children rank ordered photographs for the same duration as the practice trials. The experimental lineup was either target-present or target-absent and sequentially presented. Practice was not found to be consistently helpful and did not decrease false positive responding (in a target-absent lineup).

In Pozzulo and Lindsay's (1998) meta-analysis, sequential lineup presentation was not found to be useful in reducing false positive identification rates compared with the simultaneous lineup. Moreover, the sequential procedure appeared to increase the gap between children and adults in terms of correct rejection rates; that is, children were worse, producing fewer correct rejections, and adults were better, producing more correct rejections, when using a sequential procedure compared with a simultaneous procedure. Overall, the sequential lineup does not appear to be effective at improving the young eyewitness's identification performance.

Showups

If we reduced the number of lineup members shown to a young eyewitness to one, thereby almost forcing an absolute judgment because there are no other lineup members to consider, would a sequential process be effective for the young eyewitness? In fact, if only one lineup member was shown to the witness, could this procedure reduce false positive identifications? Such a procedure is known as a *showup*, an alternative identification procedure to a lineup. The showup procedure shows one person to the witness: the suspect. The witness is asked whether the person is the perpetrator. Although an absolute judgment is likely with a showup, there is no one to compare with to make a relative judgment; however, it has a number of difficulties, making it a less-than-ideal procedure. Both courts and researchers have argued that because there are no other lineup members shown, the witness is aware of whom the police suspect, and this knowledge may increase a witness's likelihood of making an identification that may in fact be false (*Stovall v. Denno*, 1967; Wells, Leippe, & Ostrom, 1979).

Gonzalez, Ellsworth, and Pembroke (1993) conducted a series of studies with adult participants and did not find false identifications to be higher with a showup than with a lineup. In fact, they found that adult witnesses were more likely to reject a showup than a lineup. Gonzalez et al. concluded that witnesses are more cautious in their decision making when presented with a showup rather than a lineup and, as a result, will err by making a rejection rather than an identification. Yarmey, Yarmey, and Yarmey (1996), however, reached a different conclusion: They found that lineups produced lower false identification rates than showups. In a meta-analysis comparing showups and lineups, Steblay, Dysart, Fulero, and Lindsay (2003) found that false identifications were higher with showups than with lineups. Also, in an analysis of 271 actual police cases, the suspect was more likely to be identified in a field showup (.76) than in a photographic lineup (.48; Behrman & Davey, 2001). These results are consistent with the notion that showups are suggestive and can increase the chances of a witness making an identification. What about young eyewitnesses? Could the showup up be effective at reducing false identifications when used with young eyewitnesses?

In a study that examined children, Lindsay, Pozzulo, Craig, Lee, and Corber (1997) compared simultaneous lineups, sequential lineups, and showups. Two experiments were conducted with children ages 3 to 15 years and undergraduate students. In Experiment 1 both target-present and target-absent lineups were used. Eight- to 10-year-olds, 11- to 15-year-olds, and undergraduates saw a male walk into their classroom, introduce himself, give instructions for a different study, and then exit. Participants then were informed about the lineup task. Participants were handed a package that contained a black-and-white photocopy of a six-person simultaneous lineup (simultaneous condition), a series of single pages with one photo per page (sequential condition), or a single photo (showup condition). Overall, correct identification rates did not seem to be significantly affected by the identification procedure, and this was true for each age group. In terms of correct rejection rates, adults produced higher rates than both child groups, regardless of procedure used. Children did have a higher correct rejection rate with the showup compared with the simultaneous and sequential procedure, but they also showed a tendency to guess, which can be particularly detrimental for a showup procedure because each false identification is a true false identification (i.e., there are no fillers/foils to offer the suspect protection, therefore every "pick" of an innocent suspect is a false identification).

For now, there are only two acceptable uses of a showup. It may be used for deathbed identifications, when there is a fear that the witness will not be alive by the time a lineup is assembled (Wells et al., 2000), and police may use a showup if a suspect is apprehended immediately at or near the crime scene. At this point, the showup does not appear to warrant use with young eyewitnesses (aside from the exceptions mentioned earlier).

Elimination Lineup

To develop an identification procedure for children that would maintain their correct identification rate and increase their correct rejection rate compared with adults, Pozzulo and Lindsay (1999) considered a basic question: Why do children fail at a higher rate than adults to reject target-absent lineups? One possibility is that children have more difficulty than adults with the decision-making process. Pozzulo and Lindsay suggested that the simultaneous identification task could be viewed as involving a two-judgment process. Judgment 1 determines which lineup member is most similar to the perpetrator, and Judgment 2 determines whether the most similar lineup member is, in fact, the perpetrator. They called this the two-judgment theory of identification accuracy.

Shown a lineup in which the perpetrator is present, a relative judgment leading the witness to select the most similar lineup member often produces a correct identification. Consider that the guilty party is most likely to look like him- or herself. An absolute judgment (Judgment 2) is not necessary for accuracy if the lineup foils are not overly similar to the perpetrator (see Luus & Wells, 1991; Wells et al., 1993, regarding the issue of selecting lineup distractors). Shown a lineup in which the perpetrator is absent (and the suspect is innocent), an absolute judgment is necessary for identification accuracy (i.e., correct rejection) because the most similar lineup member is not the perpetrator. In the absence of Judgment 2, a witness using a relative judgment will frequently identify an innocent lineup member (Wells, 1993).

One explanation for high rates of false positive identifications is the failure of the witness to exercise Judgment 2 in this two-judgment process. There is some evidence consistent with this hypothesis in previous eyewitness studies. As mentioned earlier, sequential lineups reduce false positive choices, perhaps by forcing witnesses to use Judgment 2 for each person in the lineup (Lindsay & Wells, 1985; Wells, 1993). Lindsay et al. (1997) found that adults who use relative judgments are responsible for a disproportionate number of false positive choices, as are those who fail to engage Judgment 2 of the identification process. Similarly, biased lineup instructions—instructions that do not inform the witness that the perpetrator may not be present but instead suggest the criminal is present, and the witness need only pick him or her out—may increase false positive identification by discouraging the use of Judgment 2 (Steblay, 1997).

There are a variety of potential reasons children may not use Judgment 2 in the identification process when presented with a simultaneous lineup. For example, children may succumb to the demands of the situation and assume that the experimenter or police officer expects an identification (Ceci, Ross, & Toglia, 1987). Once the most similar lineup member is selected, they have complied with the experimenter's or (police officer's) instructions and made an identification. There is no need for any further decision making on the part of the witness. Alternatively, children may be unaware that they should make an absolute judgment and that they should only make an identification if the most similar lineup member is actually the perpetrator. Furthermore, children may not know how to make an absolute judgment when presented with a simultaneous lineup.

If children can identify targets from target-present lineups, it would appear that they can successfully complete Judgment 1. However, as noted previously, any positive evaluation of children's identification evidence resulting from their ability to correctly identify targets is countered by the high rate of false positives with target-absent lineups. A two-judgment identification procedure that requires responses to be provided separately for each judgment rather than given as one response to the entire process may provide an opportunity for children's correct identification ability to be maintained while their false positive rate is lowered.

Pozzulo and Lindsay (1999) partitioned the simultaneous identification task into two steps corresponding to the two-judgment identification theory. First, witnesses can narrow the simultaneous lineup that contains several lineup members to the single person most similar in appearance to their memory of the perpetrator (Judgment 1). Once this individual is selected, the witness can be asked to make an identification (Judgment 2). For Judgment 2, the witness decides whether the "surviving" lineup member is or is not the perpetrator. The first step eliminates all but the lineup member most similar to the perpetrator (relative judgment), and the second step asks the witness to compare the surviving lineup member to his or her memory of the perpetrator (absolute judgment).

In the initial study that examined the "elimination procedure," Pozzulo and Lindsay (1999) took two approaches known as fast and slow elimination. With a *fast elimination* lineup, the witness is asked to select the lineup member who looks most like the target (Judgment 1). Because Pozzulo and Lindsay were not sure that children would make a distinction between selecting the lineup member most similar to the perpetrator and stating that the person so selected is not the perpetrator, a second elimination procedure was designed, namely, slow elimination. In a *slow elimination* lineup, the witness is asked to eliminate lineup members one at a time by selecting the (remaining) lineup member who looks least like the perpetrator until only one lineup member remains (Judgment 1). Two additional lineup procedures were generated by modifying the instructions for the elimination procedures that emphasized the undesirability of identifying an innocent person, and that gave direction to help the witness in making an absolute judgment. The modified instructions had previously been demonstrated to slightly increase children's correct identification rates from simultaneous lineups (Pozzulo & Lindsay, 1997). All elimination procedures (i.e., fast, fast-modified, slow, and slow-modified) were tested to examine their impact on the rates of correct identification with target-present lineups and correct rejections with target-absent lineups. These elimination procedures were compared with a simultaneous lineup and a simultaneous lineup with the same modified instructions used for the elimination procedures.

Overall, correct identification rates were fairly similar for children as a function of lineup procedure. The fast-modified elimination procedure produced a significant increase in the rate of correct rejection compared with the simultaneous procedure for children. In fact, the fast-modified elimination procedure produced a correct rejection rate for children that was similar to the correct rejection rate obtained with adults presented with a simultaneous procedure. The (fast) elimination procedure has since been studied across different age ranges and varying conditions.

For example, Pozzulo, Dempsey, and Crescini (2009) examined the identification abilities of preschool children (M_{age} = 59.10 months). Children were exposed to a female confederate for 20 minutes during a mask-making session during which the confederate walked around the room and helped all the children complete their mask. After a 20-minute delay, children were presented with either a target-absent or target-present simultaneous or elimination lineup. The researchers found that correct rejection rates were significantly higher for the elimination lineup (.80) compared with the simultaneous lineup (.52). When presented with a target-present lineup, correct identification rates were comparable for the simultaneous lineup (.44) and elimination lineup (.68). The elimination procedure seems helpful for preschoolers.

Examining older young eyewitnesses, Pozzulo, Dempsey, and Pettalia (2013) investigated identification abilities of adolescents (M_{age} = 16.49 years) and adults (M_{age} = 20.16 years) using the simultaneous, sequential, and elimination lineup procedures. Participants viewed a videotaped theft of a female's bags. After an approximate delay of 20 minutes, participants were presented with the identification task. No effects of age were found. The correct identification rates were significantly higher when participants were presented with the simultaneous lineup (.64) compared with the sequential (.41) and elimination (.45) lineups. When presented with a target-absent lineup, the elimination lineup produced the highest correct rejection rates (.72) compared with the simultaneous (.43) and sequential (.57) lineups. The elimination procedure may decrease correct identification rates while increasing correct rejection rates.

To examine the situation when a perpetrator changes his appearance following the commission of a crime, Pozzulo and Balfour (2006) examined the identification abilities of children (M_{age} = 10.41 years) and adults (M_{age} = 21.25 years) when the target changed his appearance (i.e., hairstyle and color) between the time of the crime and the identification task. Children were shown a videotape of a nonviolent theft in which a woman's purse was stolen. They were then given either a target-present or target-absent simultaneous or elimination lineup. Half the children viewed a target with no appearance change, and the other half viewed a target with an appearance change (i.e., longer and darker hair). When presented with a target-present lineup, change of appearance had a detrimental effect on both children and adults, reducing correct identification rates. Lineup procedure did not influence correct identification rates either as a function of age or appearance. A significant interaction was found between lineup procedure and appearance for correct rejection rates in that the elimination procedure was more effective at increasing the correct rejection rate when the lineup members matched the perpetrator's appearance (no change of appearance having occurred). When the lineup members did not match the perpetrator's appearance, there was no difference in the effectiveness of lineup procedures, elimination (0.61 correct rejection rate) versus simultaneous (0.67 correct rejection rate). Change of appearance is a difficult condition in which to obtain high accuracy rates. Considering modifications or alternatives to the lineup procedure may be helpful to deal with changes in appearance. Moreover, computer technology that allows for a manipulation of appearances (e.g., the addition of a baseball cap) may help improve accuracy.

Given that a number of crimes are committed by more than one perpetrator, Dempsey and Pozzulo (2013) examined whether the type of lineup procedure used influenced children's identification abilities for a two-perpetrator crime. Children (M_{age} = 10.68) viewed a nonviolent videotaped theft of CDs from a music store that involved a target and an accomplice. Participants then were given the identification task after a 25-minute delay. Each participant was given two lineups, one for the thief and one for the accomplice. When presented with a target-present lineup, the correct identifications of the thief were nonsignificantly different for the simultaneous (.28) and elimination lineups (.42); however, there was a simultaneous lineup advantage (.33) compared with the elimination lineup (.16) when participants were presented with an accomplice-present lineup. When presented with a target-absent lineup, participants were more likely to correctly reject the thief lineup when presented with an elimination lineup (.75) compared with a simultaneous lineup (.44); the correct rejection rates for the accomplice were comparable for the elimination (.60) and simultaneous (.50) lineups. Once again, some advantages for the elimination procedure can be seen; however, there may be some limits to when the elimination lineup should be used. Moreover, it is important to consider the trade-off between correct identification and correct rejection.

The elimination procedure has produced some good results with a number of older young eyewitnesses, but it also has some limitations. Further investigation of this procedure that varies the conditions that can occur in real life would be beneficial to gain a better understanding of the effectiveness of the procedure. In addition, tweaks to the procedure may produce an even more effective lineup procedure for witnesses of all ages. Certainly, there is room for improvement.

Simultaneous-Plus

Over the years, a number of researchers have attempted to modify the simultaneous procedure with the addition of a graphical representation of "not here" (e.g., a Mr. Nobody card, a silhouette, a silhouette with a superimposed question mark) to be used with young eyewitnesses to increase their correct rejection rate (e.g., Beal, Schmitt, & Dekle, 1995; Davies, Tarrant, & Flin, 1989; Karageorge & Zajac, 2011; Zajac & Karageorge, 2009).

These graphical representations are added to the simultaneous lineup presentation to give witnesses a concrete option to choose if the target/perpetrator is not there. Participants are informed that if they do not see the target in the lineup, they should select the not here/wild card graphic.

Not Here Card

Beal and colleagues (1995, Experiment 1) conducted a study in which half the participants were provided with a not here card as the method for rejecting a lineup. Kindergarten children ($M_{age} = 6.2$ years) were presented with a slide show sequence that depicted an outdoor picnic scene in which a camera was stolen. After a 5- to 7-minute delay, the children were presented with the identification task. The researchers could not definitively conclude whether the presence of the not here card facilitated a reduction in false positive identification and cautiously concluded that the card was not a major factor in a child's decision accuracy. One issue with the study was the small sample size that may, in turn, have limited what could be said about the effectiveness of the not here card.

Brewer, Keast, and Sauer (2010) conducted a study in which children, all approximately 12 years of age, were provided with a "not there" option as well as an additional "not sure" option designed to motivate them to be more accurate. Children were randomly assigned to one of three instruction conditions: control (i.e., lineup and a not there option), not sure response option (in addition to the not there option), or accuracy motivation (not there in addition to the not sure response option and extended lineup instructions). The not sure instructions indicated that if the child did not know or was not sure, it was better to click the not sure button than to guess. For the accuracy motivation condition, children were given the not sure instructions in addition to extended instructions (similar to those in Pozzulo & Lindsay, 1999) informing them that picking an innocent person could mean that the wrong person goes to jail. Also, in the motivation accuracy condition children received points for being accurate. Feedback was provided to the child after each identification decision was made (four identification decisions were made in total per participant). The researchers reported that in some conditions, the not sure option and the extended instructions helped reduce false positives. Again, the effectiveness of the options examined was somewhat unclear.

Wild Card

In another study that used a silhouette and question mark, called a *wild card* (see Figure 4.1), to provide a concrete option for children to choose if the target was not present, Zajac and Karageorge (2009) examined identification rates with 8- to 11-year-olds. Participants were exposed to a staged event at the local police station in which a police officer was discussing the role of an officer with the children. Halfway through the discussion, a confederate interrupted the police officer and asked to borrow a set of keys. Once he was given the keys, he commented that he might not be able to find the right key because of the number of keys on the key ring and then left. Following a delay of 24 to 48 hours, participants were shown either a target-present or target-absent lineup. Half the participants were told to inform the experimenter if the target was not present in the simultaneous lineup. The remaining participants were shown a simultaneous lineup that contained an additional photograph with a silhouetted figure superimposed with a question mark and were told to point to this wild

Figure 4.1

Silhouette with question mark. From "The Wildcard: A Simple Technique for Improving Children's Target-Absent Lineup Performance," by R. Zajac and A. Karageorge, 2009, *Applied Cognitive Psychology, 23*, p. 65. Copyright 2009 by Wiley. Adapted with permission.

card if the target was not present. The researchers found that the correct rejection rate was significantly higher with the wild card (.71) versus the simultaneous lineup control condition (.46). Correct identification rates (target-present lineups) did not differ significantly across conditions.

In a follow-up study, Karageorge and Zajac (2011) examined two age groups, 5- to 7-year-olds and 8- to 11-year-olds, with the use of the wild card (as in Zajac & Karageorge, 2009). Children were taken to the local fire station to learn about the role of a firefighter. When they arrived, a confederate slid down the fire pole and was reprimanded in front of the children. Children were then shown either a target-present or target-absent lineup after either a 24- to 48-hour delay or a 2-week delay. Once again, across both age groups, the wild card significantly increased correct rejections (.83) compared with the no wild card condition (.29). Correct identification rates were not influenced by the wild card inclusion.

Mystery Man

Using a representation similar to that used in the Zajac and Karageorge study (2009; Karageorge & Zajac, 2011) but called a "mystery man," Havard and Memon (2013) examined child participants 5 to 7 years old and 8 to 11 years old. A videotaped staged theft was shown to the children. Following a delay of 1 to 2 days, children were shown either a target-present or target-absent video lineup. As in a sequential lineup, each lineup member appeared as a 15-second clip, with the person looking directly into the camera, turning his or her head to the right and then to the left before returning to full face. Unlike the sequential procedure, however, the witness was shown the entire lineup twice and was not asked to make a decision for each lineup member as that member was being shown. The lineup either included a black silhouette with a white question mark or did not. Children were informed that they could verbally select one of the lineup members or the mystery man if they did not see the target. There were nine lineup members, and the mystery man appeared in the fifth position, if present. The correct identification rate did not differ across lineup procedure or age. The correct rejection rate was significantly higher when the mystery man was present than when no mystery man was included in the lineup.

The addition of a wild card certainly did not seem to hinder the young eyewitness. Does the actual representation matter? Does the look of the silhouette affect identification accuracy for the young eyewitness? Could any silhouette be used?

A Tree Outline

Along the same lines as adding a wild card or mystery man, Dunlevy and Cherryman (2013) investigated whether adding an outline of a tree could help reduce children's false positive responding. Six- to 7-year-old children engaged in a craft-making session that involved a demonstration of how to make a craft and then making the crafts themselves, after which the confederate and children sang a song together. One week later, the children took part in the identification task. Children were presented with either a target-present or target-absent simultaneous lineup or an alternative simultaneous lineup that included a tree outline. Children were instructed to choose the tree card if they believed the target was hiding behind the tree. When presented with a target-present lineup, the alternative procedure and standard procedure produced comparably accurate responses (.81 vs. .86). When presented with a target-absent lineup, children's correct rejections rates were higher in the alternative procedure (.67) compared with the standard procedure (.24). Perhaps it is more significant that an alternative is present than what that alternative is.

Zajac and Jack (2015) investigated the issue of the type of image used. They were interested in whether the physical properties of the wild card influenced children's identification abilities. Children ages 7 to 11 years old were taken to a police station for a staged event similar to the event in Zajac and Karageorge (2009). After a 1- to 2-day delay, children were presented with the identification task. Three different wild cards were examined in addition to a control: (a) a plausible wild card (consistent with the target's silhouette), (b) an implausible wild card (inconsistent with the target's silhouette), and (c) a wild card that contained a question mark. The physical appearance of the wild card did not influence correct identification rates in target-present lineups; the rates of correct identification were not significantly different across conditions. However, when presented with a target-absent lineup, the rate of correct rejections was significantly higher when the children were presented with a plausible wild card (.79) compared with no wild card (.55).

It appears that including some sort of graphical representation that implies the target is not present can be helpful to increase correct rejections for young witnesses. It also may be key that the graphical representation has some likeness to the target. A few caveats are noteworthy here, however. First, without an adult comparison group, it is hard to know whether including a graphic increases correct rejections to an adult level; however, if young eyewitnesses' accuracy is increased to above what it would be without the representation, it is beneficial. Second, because the goal of much of this eyewitness work is that it be used in the real world with real witnesses, it is important to understand what these "options" represent and whether a child is selecting this alternative to indicate that the target is not present or that they are unsure whether the target is not present. This distinction is critical in a criminal justice context because each response has different consequences for the suspect. Rejecting a lineup would suggest to police that they may have an innocent suspect, whereas a witness who is unsure of whether the perpetrator is present does not provide evidence of suspect guilt. Nonetheless, adding a graphic to a lineup procedure is a relatively simple and inexpensive option for real-life application, with the potential benefit of increasing correct rejections rates for young eyewitnesses.

CONCLUSION

Ideally, an identification procedure would be effective in increasing children's correct identification and correct rejection rates to adult level. If this procedure is useful for all ages of witnesses, the criminal justice system would not have to determine age parameters, which can be costly and require additional expertise, when administering a lineup. When compared with adults, the young eyewitness produces fewer correct identifications, as well as fewer correct rejections with the simultaneous lineup procedure (Fitzgerald & Price, 2015). However, even if an adult level of identification accuracy cannot be reached, developing a procedure that can improve the accuracy of young eyewitnesses compared with their own age group would be beneficial. The elimination procedure and the wild card method show some success over the simultaneous lineup procedure, but not sufficiently enough in their current format. Alternative procedures or modifications are needed to help young eyewitnesses improve the accuracy of their lineup decisions.

5

Other Factors Influencing the Young Eyewitness's Identification Accuracy

In addition to variables that can be manipulated after the fact, such as interview protocol and lineup procedure, a number of variables occur at the time of the crime that can have an impact on an eyewitness's testimony. This chapter focuses on four key variables that can influence the young eyewitness: arousal, whether a weapon is present, the race of the perpetrator versus witness, and own-age bias. The influence these factors have on an eyewitness is hard to estimate, and in all likelihood they interact with other variables and the system factors that occur afterward. Although these estimator variables cannot be controlled, it is important to consider their impact (Wells, 1978). Keep in mind that no one factor is solely responsible for the accuracy of an eyewitness's evidence.

http://dx.doi.org/10.1037/14956-006
The Young Eyewitness: How Well Do Children and Adolescents Describe and Identify Perpetrators?
by J. Pozzulo

AROUSAL

One factor that is likely present in all cases that involve children (and adults) is emotional arousal and stress. Arguably, some crimes can be more arousing or stressful than others. For example, crimes in which the eyewitness is also the victim may be more stressful than those in which the eyewitness was a bystander (and in particular if the eyewitness was out of harm's way). Moreover, the nature or type of some crimes is more arousing than others. Consider witnessing a parent's assault and murder versus a physical altercation between two strangers. Recall the cases discussed in Chapter 1: Kendra Lewis witnessing the murder of her mother, Mary Katherine Smart witnessing the abduction of her sister, and Kathy Sigman witnessing her friend being abducted. All these cases are on the higher end of the arousal scale. It is important to consider whether age interacts with arousal to produce an effect on memory. A number of studies have examined how stress and arousal can influence memory in general and eyewitness memory in particular. Two types of studies have been used to better understand this phenomenon: (a) studies in which arousal is manipulated in the lab or the field and (b) studies of real-life witnesses who experienced a "natural" stressful event.

Deffenbacher, Bornstein, Penrod, and McGorty (2004) reported a variety of relations found between stress/arousal and memory. In some situations, arousal can increase eyewitness accuracy—for example, when a witness says, "I was scared for my life; I will never forget that face." In other cases, stress and arousal decrease eyewitness accuracy—for example, when an eyewitness says, "I was so scared, I couldn't focus; I can't remember anything." In other cases, stress and arousal may not have much of an impact in either direction—for example, when a witness says, "I was scared, but I don't think that influenced me." Which is the case?

The Yerkes–Dodson law (YDL; Yerkes & Dodson, 1908) provides some insight into the complicated relationship between stress/arousal and memory. The YDL suggests that a moderate level of arousal provides the optimal level for best memory performance. Too much arousal or too little arousal decreases memory performance. When someone is extremely aroused, he or she may become overwhelmed and unable to focus attention and encode details for later recall or recognition. For example, some- one who is about to write a final exam might not realize that a person had walked off with someone else's laptop. When someone is experiencing low arousal, he or she may not be focusing or paying attention and again, details will not be available for recall or recognition at a later time. Con- sider someone who has just woken up and headed to the corner coffee shop for a morning coffee. This individual may not realize that the cashier is being held up. Some arousal makes you alert and able to concentrate on what is occurring for later recall or recognition. The challenge, of course, is trying to define what is considered "optimal arousal." The YDL is shown in Figure 5.1 as an inverted U function, where moderate levels of arousal result in the best memory performance.

Optimal arousal may vary depending on the context and the person and may differ depending on age. Younger witnesses may have a lower optimal threshold than adults or a higher optimal threshold, given that their ability to understand consequences and consider what may happen is not as advanced as that of adults. The direction of this interaction, if there is one, is not clear at this point. More research examining a range of ages and levels of arousal may be helpful to understand better the inter- action of age, arousal, and eyewitness memory.

Easterbrook (1959) proposed a cue-utilization hypothesis to explain why a witness may have focused attention on one detail over another. The

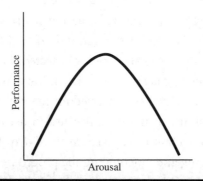

Figure 5.1

The Yerkes–Dodson law.

hypothesis suggests that when emotional arousal increases, attentional capacity decreases. With limited attentional capacity, when witnessing a crime, central details, such as the weapon, are more likely to be encoded than are peripheral details, such as the color of the perpetrator's hair. Higher levels of arousal may be more detrimental to the recall of more peripheral details of the crime and appearance of the perpetrator.

A meta-analysis by Deffenbacher et al. (2004) suggested that arousal can be construed as cognitive anxiety and somatic anxiety. *Cognitive anxiety* refers to the worry one feels, whereas *somatic anxiety* refers to one's conscious perception of physiological change (Deffenbacher et al., 2004, p. 688). Examining the influence of stress on eyewitness identification across 27 independent tests of identification abilities and the influence of stress on recall details across 36 tests, the researchers found that high levels of stress, producing both high cognitive anxiety and high somatic anxiety, can decrease eyewitness identification accuracy. Eyewitness age also was examined for any potential moderating effects. Mean proportions of correct decisions were comparable for both children and adults. The influence of heightened stress on recall was also examined. More accurate details were recalled in low-stress conditions compared with high-stress conditions. Intriguingly, age was found to be a significant moderator of the effect of stress and recall such that heightened stress was found to affect adults more negatively than children.

Some studies have examined the influence of stress on children's eyewitness identification in real-life situations. For example, Goodman, Quas, Batterman-Faunce, Riddlesberger, and Kuhn (1994) examined how experiencing a stressful medical procedure affected children's (3–10 years; M_{age} = 5.5 years) memory for the event. Participants were children ages 3 to 10 who had to have a catheter inserted for medical reasons. The study involved three sessions. In the first, parental consent and child assent were obtained. The second took place on the day of the procedure and consisted of observing and videotaping the procedure. The third session occurred after a delay (M = 11.6 days) and took place in the laboratory; children came in and took part in a memory test. Three and 4-year-olds answered significantly fewer questions correctly and made more errors compared with older children. Although the 5- to 7-year-old children made fewer correct responses than the 7- to 10-year-old children, they generally did not make more incorrect responses. A number of factors also predicted recall accuracy, including participants' understanding of the event, parental communication and emotional support, and participants' reactions. Thus, age, arousal, and individual factors can all interact to influence accuracy in recall.

Examining the identification abilities of children who experienced a stressful event, Lindberg, Jones, McComas Collard, and Thomas (2001) tested children (M_{age} = 5.05 years) who received their prekindergarten inoculations. Before the inoculations, a nurse took the child's temperature. Children were then given a shot as well as an oral inoculation from a different nurse. Children were partitioned into two groups: those who received the inoculations and those who viewed the inoculations from a distance. Both groups of children were matched on all demographic variables. After a 20-minute or 1-month delay, children were given a memory test. Children were asked to identify both the nurse who took their temperature and the nurse who administered the shots. The children who experienced the shots and those who watched others getting them were similarly accurate after the 20-minute delay. However, children who received the inoculations were more accurate in their identification decisions after a 1-month delay compared with the participants who only watched the procedure. This was true for both the nurses, suggesting that arousal and personal experience (compared with being a bystander) may be beneficial for children who later have to identify someone. When an item was peripheral to the central stressor (i.e., the shots), the control group had superior accuracy. For example, the control participants were more accurate in their recognition of the shoes worn by the nurse who took the temperature. More arousal was beneficial for some critical details, and less arousal was beneficial for less important details.

Peterson and Bell (1996) examined the influence of a naturally occurring stressful situation on identification abilities. Children were recruited from the emergency department of a hospital and were between 2 and 5 years old. Older children, ages 9 and 12 to 13, were also recruited for comparison. After a few days, children were interviewed about their emergency room visit. Stress at the time of the children's injury had less of an impact on memory than the stress children endured while interacting with the doctors who were treating them (suggesting that interview protocols may be critical when interviewing real-life young eyewitnesses). Children were able to recall details of a highly stressful situation. Older children were better able to recall more information than their younger counterparts, although accuracy was not necessarily compromised.

In another study, Fitzgerald, Price, and Connolly (2012) examined the impact of stress in a real-life situation and its influence on identification accuracy. Four- and 5-year-old children participated in either one or four swimming lessons. The swimming lessons were anxiety provoking for some of the children but not for others. Four weeks after their first (or only) lesson, children were presented with the task of identifying the swimming instructor. Anxiety was found to be unrelated to identification accuracy for both target-present and target-absent lineups at the time of the initial task. One year later, a follow-up identification task was administered. Target presence was found to influence the relationship between identification accuracy and anxiety; when presented with a target-absent lineup, anxious children made more foil identifications than correct rejections compared with the nonanxious children. Anxiety may increase children's difficulty with rejecting target-absent lineups.

Researchers have also examined the influence of stress and arousal on child eyewitnesses in a laboratory setting. Quas, Rush, Yim, and Nikolayev (2014) examined the effects of stress on memory in children (M_{age} = 7.46 years) and adolescents (M_{age} = 12.94 years). Participants took part in a two-session study. In Session 1 participants were administered the Trier Social Stress Test-Modified (TSST-M), which involves giving a speech and completing math tasks; participants were put into either a high- or low-stress condition. In the high-stress condition, participants were told that they were going to be videotaped and that this videotape would later be analyzed; in the low-stress condition, participants were told they were being videotaped for backup purposes. Session 2 took place 2 weeks later and consisted of the memory interview. Participants were assigned to either a supportive (i.e., the interviewer was dressed casually and introduced herself) or nonsupportive (i.e., the interviewer was dressed professionally and did not introduce herself) interview condition. Overall, level of stress (i.e., high vs. low) did not reliably influence memory of the experience. When examining recall accuracy, adolescents provided more information than children, as has been found in a number of other studies. Similarly, in examining recognition accuracy, adolescents provided a greater number of correct and fewer incorrect responses compared with children. This effect was more pronounced in the adolescents in the low-stress TSST-M condition. When physiological arousal was examined, children who experienced higher arousal exhibited better recall than those children who experienced lower physiological arousal. Higher arousal may have been more optimal than lower arousal.

In a similar study, Rush et al. (2014) examined the influence of stress on eyewitness accuracy with a group of 7- to 8-year-olds (M_{age} = 7.5 years) and 12- to 14-year-olds (M_{age} = 12.98 years) and also considered supportive versus nonsupportive interview conditions. When examining target-present lineups, neither age, event stress, nor interview context influenced identification accuracy. However, when examining target-absent lineups, significant effects emerged. Adolescents made significantly more correct rejections (53%) than did children, as in other studies. Across age groups, the highest rate of correct rejections occurred when participants were in the high stress and supportive interviewer conditions compared with the high stress and nonsupportive interviewer condition.

Overall, an arousing event can produce accurate recall and recognition if the eyewitness is questioned in a supportive manner. Estimator variables of age and arousal can interact with the system variables of interview protocol and interviewer. Young eyewitnesses can provide accurate testimony about a stressful event or person, provided appropriate protocols are followed.

WEAPON FOCUS

Related to arousal is *weapon focus*, the term used to describe the phenomenon of a witness's attention being focused on the perpetrator's weapon rather than on the perpetrator (Steblay, 1992). The witness will remember less about the crime and perpetrator when a weapon is present than when no weapon is present. It is clear that this phenomenon occurs, but why it occurs is less clear. There have been two primary explanations for the weapon focus effect: arousal and unusualness.

Davies, Smith, and Blincoe (2008) examined whether the weapon focus effect impaired children's identification abilities to the same degree as in adults. Three groups of children were examined: 3-year-olds, 4-year-olds, and 5-year-olds. Children were presented with an array of 14 common objects (e.g., a coin, leaf, tissue); those in the experimental condition saw among those a syringe filled with red food dye. In two other conditions, the syringe was replaced with either a phone or pen. Children were given approximately 40 seconds to look at the items before they would no longer be able to view them. Children were then asked to recall how many items they remembered seeing. After a 3-hour delay, children were asked questions about the experimenter's appearance. Participants who viewed the syringe in the array of common objects had the poorest performance in recalling the experimenter's appearance ($M = 5.33$ out of 10 details) compared with participants who saw the phone array ($M = 6.75$) and pen array ($M = 6.55$). No differences were found between the phone and pen arrays. These results suggest that participants spent a disproportionate amount of time on the syringe. Interestingly, no effects of age were found.

As previously mentioned, the cue-utilization hypothesis proposed by Easterbrook (1959) explained why a witness may focus on the weapon rather than other details. The hypothesis suggests that when emotional arousal increases, attentional capacity decreases. With limited attentional capacity, central details such as the weapon, are more likely to be encoded than are peripheral details. An alternative explanation for the weapon focus phenomenon has to do with unusualness: weapons are unusual and thus attract a witness's attention. Because a witness is not paying attention to and encoding other details, these other details are not remembered (Mitchell, Livosky, & Mather, 1998; Pickel, 1998). Following this line of thinking, one would predict that other objects might produce a weapon focus effect if they were unusual in the situation.

Pickel (1999) conducted two experiments to investigate the unusualness explanation. In one of the experiments, university students watched one of four videotapes in which a woman was approached by a man with a handgun. The scenarios differed in their location and the degree of threat posed to the witness. In one video, the interaction occurred at a baseball game in the stadium parking lot. In the other video, the interaction occurred at a shooting range. The handgun is unusual at the baseball game, whereas it is not unusual at the shooting range. In the low-threat condition, the man kept the gun pointed to the ground. In the high-threat condition, the man pointed the gun at the woman. Participants provided less accurate descriptions of the man if he was carrying a gun in the parking lot rather than at the shooting range. The degree of threat did not influence the description of the man. These data suggest that unusualness can produce the weapon focus phenomenon. However, it should be noted that identification of the target was not affected.

In keeping with the notion of unusualness, Carlson and Carlson (2012) examined whether a perpetrator with a distinctive facial feature would alter the weapon focus effect. A total of 600 participants watched a mock-crime video in which the perpetrator used his fists, a beer bottle, or a shotgun in an apparent assault. The perpetrator either had a large sports sticker on his face or did not. Participants had more difficulty identifying the perpetrator when he had a shotgun—the weapon focus effect—but only if the perpetrator did not have a sticker on his face. When the perpetrator had a sticker on his face, correct identifications increased and false positive identifications decreased in the shotgun condition. These results suggest that an interaction may occur between the appearance of the target and whether a weapon is present. How does the weapon-focus-unusualness hypothesis apply to the young eyewitness?

Pickel, Narter, Jameson, and Lenhardt (2008) examined whether the weapon focus effect generalizes to children when they are asked to describe a target. Young children (ages 4 and 5), school-age children (ages 7 and 8), and undergraduate students viewed a videotape segment depicting a birthday party. The target brought a delivery to the party. He was depicted as either a chef or mail carrier. Once he entered the house, he was seen holding either a knife or water bottle. The role of the target varied to determine whether the weapon focus effect is driven by unusualness (i.e., when something goes against one's schema). Overall, 4- and 5-year-old children had lower accuracy scores than the 7- and 8-year-old children. Both age groups were less accurate than the undergraduate students. Recall accuracy was found to be lower for the target when he was carrying the knife compared with when he was carrying a water bottle. There was also an interaction of schema role and the object the target was carrying, suggesting unusualness may drive the weapon focus effect. Participants who viewed the mail carrier target holding a knife had lower accuracy scores than those who viewed the mail carrier holding the water bottle; accuracy scores for those who viewed the chef were similar when he was holding the knife or the water bottle. When examining these results by age, the 4- and 5-year-old children were more influenced when the mail carrier was carrying the knife, such that they had lower accuracy scores than the 7- and 8-year-olds and undergraduate students. These results suggest that the weapon focus effect can, and does, generalize to children.

Overall, there is support for the unusualness explanation for the weapon focus effect, and it seems to apply to the young eyewitness as well. In a meta-analysis of the weapon focus effect, Fawcett, Russell, Peace, and Christie (2013) found the effect to occur not only in lab studies but also in real-world investigations. It is important to note that other estimator and/or system variables may affect the degree to which the weapon focus occurs. More research is needed to definitively conclude why the weapon focus effect occurs and its influence on young eyewitnesses. It may be encouraging to know that Pickel, Ross, and Truelove (2006) found that participants could be trained not to focus on a weapon, thus reducing the weapon focus effect. Perhaps the young eyewitness could also be trained to reduce the weapon focus effect. Similarly, particular interview protocols may be effective at reducing the weapon focus effect.

CROSS-RACE IDENTIFICATION

The *cross-race effect*, also known as the *other-race effect* and the *own-race bias*, is the phenomenon of witnesses remembering faces of people of their own race with greater accuracy than they remember faces of people of other races (Malpass & Kravitz, 1969; Meissner & Brigham, 2001).

In a meta-analysis, Meissner and Brigham (2001) examined 30 years of research including almost 5,000 participants. They found that own-race faces produced higher correct identifications and lower false positives than other-race faces. This cross-race effect has been reported with adult witnesses in field studies (e.g., Brigham, Maass, Snyder, & Spaulding, 1982; Platz & Hosch, 1988) as well as in laboratory studies (Meissner & Brigham, 2001; Sporer, 2001a).

A number of studies have examined the young eyewitness and cross-race identification. For example, a study by Feinman and Entwisle (1976) was one of the first to examine the cross-race effect in children. Participants were Black and White children in Grades 1, 2, 3, and 6; identification accuracy of same- and other-race faces was examined. Children were presented with a series of 20 Black and White faces in the learning phase and were later presented with an additional 20 Black and White faces and were asked to determine whether a face had been previously seen. Both Black and White children recognized same-race faces more accurately than other-race faces; however, Black children were better at recognizing White faces than White children were at recognizing Black faces. Overall facial recognition significantly increased with each grade level; however, this increase then leveled off around Grade 3.

In another face recognition study that included an adult comparison, Chance, Turner, and Goldstein (1982) examined the ability to recognize same- and other-race faces among Caucasian first and second graders, fifth and sixth graders, seventh and eighth graders, and undergraduate students. Participants first engaged in the study phase, which consisted of viewing a set of 16 White or Japanese faces. They then immediately engaged in the recognition phase that consisted of viewing the original 16 photos intermixed with 48 new photographs. Four to 7 days later, participants engaged in the same tasks as in the first session but with the opposite race. Children in Grades 1 and 2 did not significantly differ in the recognition abilities of same- and other-race faces; however, the remaining age groups all elicited higher same-race recognition compared with other-race recognition, suggesting that the cross-race effect does increase with age. Recall in Chapter 4 that (same race) correct identification rates also seem to increase with age.

Kask and Bull (2009, Experiment 1) examined the influence of target race on recognition accuracy in children (M_{age} = 9 years, 2 months) and adults (M_{age} = 17.5 years). Participants were shown a series of four target faces: Caucasian, African American, Turkish, Latino, or Chinese, to represent a real-life situation in which multiple ethnicities are encountered. The targets were visible to participants for 30 seconds; after a short delay participants viewed a series of 30 test faces presented sequentially. Two of the target faces were among the 30 faces seen; these were labeled as target-present conditions. The remaining two faces were not among the 30 test faces, and this was labeled as the target-absent condition. Same-race faces were more often correctly rejected than were other-race faces in the target-absent conditions. When examining the target-present conditions, participants made comparable hits for same-race and other-race faces; similarly, false identification rates were comparable for same-race and other-race faces. Adults made significantly fewer false identifications for same-race faces than other-race faces; however, children produced comparable rates. Adults also falsely identified same-race faces more so than children. Accuracy in correctly identifying other-race faces may have a greater impact in target-absent lineups than target-present lineups. The young eyewitness may have even greater difficulty with other-race faces when examining a target-absent lineup; however, the pattern is not consistent. There may be other factors that affect this relation. Age itself may influence identification accuracy differentially across the young eyewitness.

Corenblum and Meissner (2006) examined the cross-race effect in White Canadian children in Grades 2 through 4 (M_{age} = 9.21 years), Grades 5 and 6 (M_{age} = 11.09 years), and Grades 7 and 8 (M_{age} = 12.79 years) and undergraduate students (M_{age} = 20.03 years). Participants first saw 24 Black and White adult faces during the encoding phase. After a 10-minute delay, participants underwent the test phase, which consisted of seeing the previously shown 24 faces among 24 foils. Participants, regardless of age, were more accurate in identifying the faces of their own race (.69) versus faces of a different race (.60). Although there were more hits for other-race faces (.59) than same-race faces (.42), there were higher rates of false alarms for other-race faces (.45) compared with same-race faces (.19).

Experiment 2 enlisted White Canadian children in Grades 2 through 4 (M_{age} = 8.83 years), Grades 5 and 6 (M_{age} = 10.68 years), Grades 7 and 8 (M_{age} = 12.47 years), and undergraduate students (M_{age} = 20.39 years). The procedure was similar to Experiment 1; however, another racial group was added to the photographs. Participants were now presented with White, Black, or Native Canadian faces. Consistent with Experiment 1, faces of the same-race were more accurately recognized (.79) than African American faces (.73) and Native Canadian faces (.77). As in Experiment 1, more hits were made in response to African American faces (.72) and Native Canadian faces (.74) than same-race faces (.48). Undergraduate students made significantly more hits (.75) than children in Grades 2 through 4 (.56). False alarms were significantly higher for African American photographs (.41) than for Native Canadian photographs (.35); furthermore, more false alarms were observed for Native Canadian photographs than for White photographs. The results of these two studies support the robustness of the cross-race effect across different stimuli with different ages.

Pezdek, Blandon-Gitlin, and Moore (2003) examined the cross-race effect in kindergarten children (M_{age} = 5.63 years), third graders (M_{age} = 8.63 years), and young adults (M_{age} = 24.61 years). Participants viewed a 2.5-minute video of a cooking show with one Black man and one White man. The test phase occurred the following day and consisted of a video of a six-person all-White or all-Black lineup for each target; each lineup member stood forward for a 15-second headshot. White participants were more accurate in identifying the White target (.74) than the Black target (.68), and Black participants were more accurate in identifying the Black target (.81) than the White target (.66). For each age group, same-race recognition accuracy was higher than other-race recognition accuracy. In addition, there was an effect of age, with the highest recognition accuracy in adults (.80), followed by the third graders (.77), and the kindergarten children (.62).

Cross-race researchers have examined a variety of races. For example, Sporer, Trinkl, and Guberova (2007) examined the cross-race effect among Turkish and Austrian children (ages 10–15) for German and Turkish faces with a perceptual matching task. Children were given the task of viewing

10 frontal photographs of either same-race or other-race faces for 30 seconds. Children then participated in a matching task in which they were asked to match the faces previously seen with new photographs of the same people presented in a three-quarters profile view. Austrian children took longer to match Turkish faces (M = 55.85 seconds) than German faces (M = 39.35). Similarly, Turkish children took longer to match Turkish faces (M = 48.9) than German faces (M = 39.9), but the difference in time between the two sets of faces was smaller compared with the Austrian children. Grade level was also examined (Grades, 5, 6, 7, 8) and was found to be significant. Fifth graders (M = 42.6) took longer than sixth graders (M = 39.5), seventh graders (M = 39.2), and eighth graders (M = 37.1); the difference between fifth and sixth graders differed reliably. Interestingly, no evidence was found for the cross-race effect increasing with age.

Goodman and colleagues (2007) examined the cross-race effect in a multi-nation study with children from the United States, Norway, and South Africa. Participants were 5- to 7-year-olds (M_{age} = 5 years, 10 months), 9- to 10-year-olds (M_{age} = 9 years, 3 months), 12- to 13-year-olds (M_{age} = 12 years, 3 months), and undergraduate students. The study session consisted of viewing 12 pictures (four White, four Asian, four African), and after a 2-day delay being tested with a total of 48 pictures (12 old, 36 new). The pictures consisted of 16 White faces, 16 Asian faces, and 16 African faces. As in previous research, same-race faces were more accurately recognized than other-race faces. There was an overall effect of age, with 5- to 7-year-olds displaying significantly lower recognition accuracy than the school children, adolescents, and young adults. Interestingly, the youngest children did not display the typical cross-race effect; their accuracy scores were comparable for same-race faces and other-race faces. However, the school-age children, adolescents, and undergraduate students all displayed the effect and were not significantly different from each other. Once children reached 10 to 12 years of age, they approached the adult skill level in remembering new faces. When examining false alarm rates, participants had higher rates for other-race faces than same-race faces. Significantly more false alarms for other-race faces were evident at each age group. When examining same-race false alarms, school-age children made significantly fewer false alarms than the other age groups.

Adding another estimator variable to the mix, Pezdek and Stolzenberg (2014) examined whether familiarity of a face is diagnostic of prior contact and whether the accuracy in these familiarity judgments is affected by the cross-race effect (i.e., the finding that individuals are better at identifying members of their own race than a different race; Meissner & Brigham, 2001). To examine familiarity, White and Asian high school sophomores were recruited from two different schools (M_{age} = 15.32 years, n = 75 for School A; M_{age} = 15.37 years, n = 64 for School B). Participants were initially presented with 40 yearbook photos of familiar and unfamiliar faces of students who had graduated the year before; similarly, target race was varied between White and Asian (Pezdek & Stolzenberg, 2014). Familiar faces from one school served as the unfamiliar faces for the other school. In the test phase, participants were presented with 20 photos of White students (10 familiar, 10 unfamiliar) and 20 photos of Asian students (10 familiar, 10 unfamiliar) and were asked whether each face had been seen before. The overall false alarm rate of incorrectly identifying an unfamiliar face as familiar was lower than the overall hit rate of correctly identifying a familiar face as familiar. A participant's familiarity judgment was diagnostic of prior contact; however, Pezdek and Stolzenberg concluded that it has little forensic utility because the overall hit rate was relatively low. When examining whether the cross-race effect was evident for adolescent witnesses, Pezdek and Stolzenberg found that White participants were more accurate in recognizing same-race faces than other-race faces, thus supporting the cross-race effect in adolescents. Asian participants were equally likely to accurately recognize same- and other-race faces. Thus, the cross-race effect does not necessarily occur for all races.

The cross-race effect seems to occur from 5 years of age to adulthood. That is, own-race faces are more accurately identified than cross-race faces across the ages. Also intriguing is that the size of the cross-race effect does not seem to vary as a function of age (Pezdek et al., 2003). Why does the cross-race effect occur? Different hypotheses consider the role of attitudes, physiognomic homogeneity, and interracial contact.

Attitudes

One hypothesis explaining the cross-race effect is based on attitudes. Specifically, people with fewer prejudicial attitudes may be more inclined to distinguish among members of other races. However, research to date does not support this explanation (Platz & Hosch, 1988; Slone, Brigham, & Meissner, 2000). Having said that, Meissner and Brigham (2001) did note that prejudicial attitudes might be related to the amount of contact a person has with other-race members, which in turn, may help to explain the other-race effect.

Physiognomic Homogeneity

An alternative explanation of the cross-race effect is that some races have less variability in their faces—that is, "they all look alike." This hypothesis has not received much empirical support. Goldstein, Johnson, and Chance (1979), for example, examined Japanese, Black, and White faces and did not find that one group was more similar across members than were others. Although physical similarity may not explain the cross-race effect, some physical features, such as hair color, may be more appropriate for discriminating among faces of certain races (Deregowski, Ellis, & Shepherd, 1975; Shepherd & Deregowski, 1981). Thus, persons from other races may not pay attention or encode relevant features that distinguish between members of a particular race. For example, paying attention to hair color for Asian faces may be less discriminating than hair color for Caucasian faces. This explanation, however, does not seem adequate for explaining the cross-race phenomenon.

Interracial Contact

The hypothesis perhaps receiving the most attention examines the amount or type of contact people have had with other races. This hypothesis states that the more contact one has with other races, the better one will be able to identify members of those races. In the 1970s, some researchers examined children and adolescents living in integrated neighborhoods versus those living in segregated neighborhoods. It was predicted that participants from integrated neighborhoods would be better at recognizing other-race faces than would those living in segregated neighborhoods. Some support for this predication was found (Cross, Cross, & Daly, 1971; Feinman & Entwisle, 1976).

In a related vein, de Heering, de Liedekerke, Deboni, and Rossion (2010) examined the cross-race effect in 6- to 14-year-old Asian children who were adopted into Caucasian families when they were between 2 and 26 months of age, along with a group of age-matched Caucasian children. The children went through two phases: They saw 10 Caucasian and Asian faces in the learning phase and the same 10 faces paired with a new face for the recognition phase. Results showed that Caucasian children showed a clear cross-race effect; Caucasian children showed higher hit rates with same-race faces than other-race faces. Interestingly, Asian children who were adopted into Caucasian families did not exhibit the cross-race effect, hit rates were comparable for both same-race and other-race faces. No influence of age was found.

It is important to note that not all studies that have investigated interracial contact have found the predicted effect. For example, Ng and Lindsay (1994) examined university students from Canada and Singapore, and the other-race effect was not completely supported. A definitive conclusion on the contact hypothesis and how it factors into the cross-race effect across age remains unclear.

OWN-AGE BIAS

This chapter would be remiss without discussing one often obvious but overlooked issue, namely, that the young eyewitness is often in a different "age cohort" than the perpetrator. As in the cross-race effect, is it easier for witnesses to identify perpetrators from a similar age cohort. Will a 21-year-old witness be more accurate at identifying a 25-year-old than a 10-year-old trying to describe and identify a 25-year-old? If the perpetrator was 12 years old, would a young eyewitness be more accurate at describing and identifying the 12-year-old than would a 25-year-old eyewitness?

The majority of eyewitness research involving young eyewitnesses has used a target falling outside the age cohort (i.e., older than 10 years) of the young eyewitness (e.g., eyewitness is 8 years old, and the target/confederate/perpetrator is 21 years old). As such, it is important to consider findings with this potential bias in mind (if it in fact exists). A bias may exist if one can more accurately identify a target within one's own age cohort. The majority of the research that has been conducted into own-age bias has used more standard facial recognition designs (in contrast to eyewitness designs; e.g., Anastasi & Rhodes, 2005, 2006; Bäckman, 1991; Bartlett & Leslie, 1986; Fulton & Bartlett, 1991).

In one such study, Anastasi and Rhodes (2005) examined an own-age bias in face recognition for children (5–8 years) and older adults (55–89 years) by showing participants 32 photographs and having the participants categorize the faces into one of four age ranges (5–8, 18–25, 35–45, 55–75 years). After the encoding phase, a 5-minute delay was imposed. After the delay, participants were presented with a recognition task. During the recognition task, participants were shown 64 photographs and told that some of the individuals presented would be the same individuals who had been presented previously. Participants were asked to indicate whether each individual who was presented had been presented earlier or was new. Results from that study are consistent with an own-age bias. Both older adults and children exhibited higher levels of facial recognition for individuals in their own age cohort compared with individuals from other age groups.

In another study, List (1986) examined the potential for a target-age bias by comparing the recognition abilities of 10-year-olds, college-age students (no specific ages were given) and older adults (65–70-year-olds). Participants viewed several shoplifting videos in which the perpetrators were either college-age or middle-age women (no specific ages for the perpetrators were given). Results indicated that older adults had poorer recognition memory for the college-age perpetrators, but older adults were more accurate at recognizing the middle-age perpetrators. Although these results are suggestive of an own-age bias, various methodological issues prevent the results from being considered conclusive. For example, the ages of the culprits depicted in the video were not the same age group as participants.

D. B. Wright and Stroud (2002, Experiment 2) attempted to examine further the influence of the relative ages of the witness and perpetrator on eyewitness accuracy. Younger (18–33 years old) and older (40–55 years old) adults each viewed four crime videos: two videos depicting the theft of a car in which the thief was either a 23-year-old or 51-year-old man and two videos depicting the theft of a television in which the thief was either a 21-year-old or 48-year-old man. The next day, participants were asked to complete descriptions for each of the four criminals. Participants were then shown four lineups (one for each criminal) in the same order as they saw the crime videos. Results indicated that when the target was present in the lineup, a target-age bias occurred; that is, young witnesses were more accurate when identifying a young perpetrator and less accurate when identifying an older perpetrator. Similarly, older witnesses were more accurate when identifying an older perpetrator and less accurate when identifying a younger perpetrator. No age bias was observed; however, when the target was not included in the lineup—that is, when participants were presented with a target-absent lineup—they were equally likely to correctly reject the lineup, regardless of the perpetrator's age.

In a study that more closely resembles traditional eyewitness research studies, Pozzulo and Dempsey (2009a) had adults (M_{age} = 19.34 years) attempt to identify either a child target (age 11) or an adult target (age 22). The targets were each filmed taking a woman's purse trying in videos that mirrored each other such that only the target differed. Correct identification rates were higher for the child target than the adult target, but correct rejection rates were higher for the adult target than the child target. Witnesses were more likely to select a lineup member than reject the lineup when presented with the child rather than the adult target. It is intriguing to speculate that adults perhaps become more unsure when the target is outside their age range. Possibly, young eyewitnesses also become more unsure when attempting to identify someone outside their age range. Speculating further, it may be less about memory for a target than memory for other influences that can interact with identification decisions, such as the social dynamics of the situation or unease with unfamiliar tasks.

Rhodes and Anastasi (2012) conducted a comprehensive review of own-age bias and found there were indeed greater hits and fewer false alarms for same-age faces than other-age faces. Moreover, discriminability, the ability to discriminate between faces seen before versus new faces, was better for same-age rather than other-age faces. It is important to note that the majority of these studies could be classified as "face recognition studies" that involve a number of targets and several trials per participant, unlike more traditional eyewitness research with one target and one trial or lineup per participant. Also, relatively few studies examining the own-age bias have been conducted with child participants. Why does the own-age bias effect occur? Different theories examine the role of experience, perceptual learning, and social–cognitive learning.

Experience-Based Explanations

The most popular theory for the own-age bias is that people are better at recognizing others within their own age cohort because of their increased experience with others within this cohort. There is good support for this theory; in fact, any studies reporting an own-age bias, including those described previously, could suggest that the bias was at least partially related to greater experience with a particular age group. He, Ebner, and Johnson (2011) presented participants with faces, either own-age or different-age, and measured the amount of time each face was studied. They also asked for self-reports of the amount of exposure participants had to own-age and other-age people. They later had participants identify faces as old (i.e., previously seen) or new. The length of time spent studying a face was significantly longer for own-age faces and was linked to the accuracy of categorizing faces as old or new. The amount of self-report exposure also predicted, independently, level of accuracy: More exposure was linked to higher accuracy.

He et al. suggested that there were more accessible "schemas" (i.e., abstract knowledge structures that are temporally and spatially organized and that assist in the identification of typical or reoccurring actions, actors, and props associated with any instance of a specific event; Farrar & Goodman, 1992; Lampinen, Copeland, & Neuschatz, 2011) for own-age faces, which would arise with perceptual learning.

Does prior experience influence own-age bias? That is, do older people display less own-age bias because of prior experience with other-age cohorts? Alternatively, does only recent experience contribute to own-age bias? Some studies have found that only younger adults display own-age bias, not older adults. For example, Wiese, Schweinberger, and Hansen (2008) found that young participants showed a heightened ability to recognize own-age faces in comparison with other faces, whereas elderly participants did not demonstrate such a difference. This supports the idea that prior experience could mitigate own-age bias. However, in their meta-analysis of studies involving own-age bias, Rhodes and Anastasi (2012) specifically addressed these two questions and found that own-age bias was consistently demonstrated in all age groups. They therefore concluded that only recent experience plays a role in own-age bias.

Perceptual Learning Versus Social–Cognitive Theories

Perceptual learning is the process of improving perceptual skills (i.e., skills related to any of our five senses). The perceptual learning theory for own-age bias is driven by the evidence that, as just described, experience appears to play a major role in accounting for own-age bias. In other words, the more exposure someone has to faces of his or her own age, the better he or she becomes at recognizing faces from his or her age group because of repeated exposure.

In contrast to the perceptual learning theory, a social–cognitive theory for own-age bias suggests that people categorize faces by whether they belong to a person's in-group, which in this case would be his or her own age group. This is related to Sporer's (2001b) in-group/out-group model of face processing, which posits that when people are shown an in-group face (in our case, an own-age face), they can quickly categorize it as belonging to their in-group because of expertise with such faces and having more mental resources to focus on individual features that differentiate that face from other faces. However, if they are presented with a face from an out-group, they have to spend more time determining what category it fits into and, therefore, they have fewer mental resources to process the specific features that differentiate that face from others.

Much research has suggested that younger people's attitudes toward members of their own age group differ from their attitudes toward people from other age groups. For example, D. B. Wright and Loftus (2008) found that when participants were asked to rate faces on a scale from very negative to very positive, the younger participants rated younger faces more positively than older faces, whereas older participants did not differ in their ratings of the young and old faces. In their meta-analysis of the own-age bias effect, Rhodes and Anastasi (2012) examined both theories and suggested that a more accurate account of own bias would likely include elements of both the perceptual learning and social–cognitive theories. There is definitely room for future research in this area.

CONCLUSION

This chapter focused on estimator variables and their impact on identification accuracy, as mediated by age. Perhaps most striking is that no estimator variable operates independently of other factors. We have also seen that system variables can influence the impact of estimator variables. The exact degree to which estimator variables exert an impact on eyewitness recall and identification is unclear. Some variables may increase accuracy; for example, in some stressful situations, accuracy may be improved. In other cases, accuracy may be decreased; for example, in some instances when an eyewitness is describing and identifying a perpetrator who is of a different race. Furthermore, in other instances, some factors may have no influence on accuracy. For example, the weapon focus has not consistently been found to negatively affect identification accuracy. Research should examine estimator variables in combination with the system variables that may help to reduce or eliminate any negative impact of the estimator variable(s).

6

Why Recall and Identification Abilities Differ Between Young and Adult Eyewitnesses

Up to this point, the majority of this book has focused on young eyewitnesses' recall and recognition abilities, but I have also noted how these abilities differ from those of adult eyewitnesses. Why do these differences exist? Perhaps if we can understand the "why," it may help guide us on how to obtain the most accurate evidence possible. This chapter examines why differences in recall and recognition may occur between young eyewitnesses and adult eyewitnesses.

RECALL: ARE CHILDREN REALLY LESS ACCURATE THAN ADULTS?

As discussed in Chapter 2, young eyewitnesses have less complete recall than adults, but the accuracy of their recall might be no less than that of adults. To understand why this may be the case, I next describe the fundamental

http://dx.doi.org/10.1037/14956-007
The Young Eyewitness: How Well Do Children and Adolescents Describe and Identify Perpetrators?
by J. Pozzulo

mechanisms of memory and the central developmental theory for memory, namely, the fuzzy trace theory (Brainerd & Reyna, 2005). This section also highlights the possibility of developmental reversals, in which young eyewitnesses may be more accurate than adult eyewitnesses.

Mechanisms of Memory

Memory can be understood as consisting of three steps: encoding, storage, and retrieval. *Encoding* refers to the process of taking new information or stimuli and converting that information into a memory. Information can be encoded into memory in a number of different ways. Research has found that *semantic encoding* (i.e., understanding and relating the meaning of new information to previously stored information) is the most successful type of encoding (S. C. Brown & Craik, 2000; Craik & Tulving, 1975; Mondani, Pellegrino, & Battig, 1973). Information that is encoded is later consolidated into short- or long-term memory and can then be retrieved.

Recall memory is a specific memory technique involved in the retrieval of information. Recall (along with recognition) is a process in which we can remember or retrieve previously encoded and stored stimuli. As mentioned previously, for information to be recalled, it must first have been encoded and stored in working memory, short-term memory, or long-term memory. When information is encoded, individuals may be explicitly aware that they are doing so, or they may encode information incidentally (Marschark & Hunt, 1989; Mondani et al., 1973; A. Parker, Dagnall, & Munley, 2012). *Explicit encoding* refers to situations in which individuals know they are supposed to learn and later remember specific information— for example, when studying for a test or learning a word list. *Implicit encoding* occurs when individuals are unaware that they will be later asked to recall information. This may occur in the context of a crime, where eyewitnesses are later asked to recall what a perpetrator looks like. Similarly, information can be explicitly or incidentally retrieved from memory (Challis, Velichkovsky, & Craik, 1996; Clarke & Butler, 2008; A. Parker et al., 2012). More on techniques to improve recall can be found in Chapter 3.

Fuzzy Trace Theory of Recall Memory

Theories of recall memory provide a framework for understanding children's recall capabilities, which can later be tested and applied to children's eyewitness recall in the context of the justice system. A key developmental memory theory that may help understand person descriptions provided by the young eyewitness is the *fuzzy trace theory* (FTT; Brainerd & Reyna, 2005). FTT is a dual-processing model of memory that can be used to explain memory processing. It provides a structure in which to understand the effects of time and age on recall memory. FTT is based on an opponent-processing model of memory that suggests that memories are observed, processed, and retrieved using two processes. These two processes work in parallel (i.e., encode information simultaneously from the same stimuli) but in different (i.e., opposing) ways. Memory representations are encoded from experiences, and the two processes can be explained as either verbatim or gist traces. *Verbatim* traces can be understood as representations of item-specific information (i.e., memory for what actually happens; Brainerd & Reyna, 2005). *Gist* traces, however, can be understood as semantic memory, or "relational, and elaborative information" (Brainerd & Reyna, 2004, p. 84). Gist retrieval is a broader, more general form of remembering. Both verbatim and gist traces are derived from the same stimuli; however, the way in which verbatim and gist traces are stored and retrieved differ.

It is through the storage and retrieval of verbatim or gist traces that we can understand recall memory, such that reliance on verbatim traces relative to gist traces can increase or decrease recall performance. Put simply, verbatim traces are hypothesized to result in more accurate memory recall because specific information is being activated, in contrast to general information activated in gist traces (Reyna & Kiernan, 1994).

Verbatim and gist traces also differ in their "lifespan," such that verbatim memory develops more quickly than gist memory (Brainerd & Reyna, 1995). The connections between detailed and broad information (verbatim and gist knowledge) tend to take longer to develop, suggesting that young children rely more heavily on verbatim memory during recall. Furthermore, gist traces are more likely to strengthen over time, whereas verbatim traces are more likely to weaken or deteriorate over time (Brainerd & Reyna, 1998, 2004), resulting in a heavier reliance on gist memory as one ages.

The improvement of gist memory with age suggests that memory errors are also more likely to increase with age (e.g., Brainerd & Reyna, 2005, 2015). This contradicts some previous work suggesting that children make more memory errors than adults (Brainerd & Reyna, 2015). Indeed, some research has found that as children age, increases in memory errors were found when the to-be-remembered information was semantically related (i.e., it had a shared meaning; e.g., Ceci, Papierno, & Kulkofsky, 2007; Connolly & Price, 2006; Dewhurst & Robinson, 2004). Adults' reliance on gist traces and ability to connect meaning between to-be-remembered stimuli suggests that they may be more susceptible to memory errors than are children (Brainerd, Forrest, Karibian, & Reyna, 2006; Brainerd & Reyna, 2007).

The development of gist and verbatim traces with age provides a framework to understand children's recall memory when they are eyewitnesses to a crime. According to the FTT framework, the underdeveloped gist trace memory in young children suggests that children are less likely to make memory errors when recalling a crime than are adult eyewitnesses. Studies examining children's eyewitness recall have found that children can be as accurate as adults when asked to recall details (e.g., Jack, Leov, & Zajac, 2014; Pozzulo & Warren, 2003), suggesting that child eyewitnesses can often provide valuable and accurate information after witnessing a crime.

LINEUP IDENTIFICATION: WHY ARE CHILD WITNESSES LESS RELIABLE THAN ADULT WITNESSES?

We have seen that the young eyewitness is capable of correctly identifying the perpetrator and rejecting a lineup that does not contain the perpetrator. However, these abilities are not comparable with those of adults. Adults have been found to produce more accurate correct identifications and correct rejections than young eyewitnesses. Understanding why there is a difference between young and adult eyewitnesses may reveal how we should best obtain identification evidence from young eyewitnesses. This section explores the explanations that have been put forth to understand differences in identification decisions between young and adult eyewitnesses.

Memory

Developmental differences in attending to or encoding a target's face may exist such that memory trace strength for faces increases with age (Diamond & Carey, 1977; Nelson & Kosslyn, 1976). A number of studies have shown a developmental increase in identifying previously seen faces (Chance & Goldstein, 1984; Fitzgerald & Price, 2015). Assuming a child's memory trace may be weaker than that of an adult, the target in a target-present lineup may serve as a sufficient cue for the child in some instances. The target in a target-present lineup is the source of the memory and thus the lineup member who most closely matches the child's memory. This match between the memory and target leads to a correct identification. When witnesses are presented with a target-absent lineup, a weaker memory trace may allow a lower criterion for a match to be made; thus, an innocent lineup member is more readily identified. There are instances when children's memory is insufficient for correct identification as well as correct rejection. Thus, there may be differences in attention, encoding, retrieval, and so forth between children and adults, with these factors improving with age (and then perhaps declining into older age). A related construct that may lead to differential identification patterns between children and adults pertains to how a face is processed. Do children and adults encode and process a face differently?

Processing Strategy

How we encode or process a face may differ between children and adults. A *featural* or piecemeal approach is used when we focus on individual features and encode them in isolation. In contrast, a *holistic* approach is used when we encode the features and the relations between the features to produce a more complete or holistic image.

Bower and Karlin (1974) studied depth of processing and its relation to facial recognition. Twelve university students were recruited as participants and asked to either (a) assign a sex of male or female to the person in a photograph, (b) rate the person in the photograph subjectively with respect to likeability, or (c) rate the person subjectively with regard to honesty. Participants had 5 seconds to process the faces. The participants were then shown a new set of slides, which contained some slides that had already been presented. Participants had to identify slides as either new (i.e., not in original set) or old (i.e., already seen in original set). Bower and Karlin found that participants did not remember the pictures that had been judged only as male or female as well as those that had been rated for likeability or honesty. Bower and Karlin concluded that when making judgments of likeability or honesty, more features were likely examined than when making a simple judgment of sex; this would involve a greater depth of processing and, in turn, enable recognition of the face later on.

Facial recognition studies provide evidence of higher identification accuracy when a holistic strategy (i.e., configural processing) is used to encode the face rather than if individual features are focused on (i.e., featural processing; Bower & Karlin, 1974; Wells & Hryciw, 1984; Winograd, 1976). Studies of facial recognition have claimed that children under the age of 10 represent faces in memory primarily by featural information (Carey & Diamond, 1977; Diamond & Carey, 1977). Conversely, it is believed that adults represent faces in memory primarily by configural information (e.g., spatial layout of elements within a face; Tanaka & Farah, 1993). Diamond and Carey (1977) conducted an experiment in which children ages 6 to 16 were shown three photographs and asked which of the two photographs in the bottom row was of the same person as the one in the top row. There were four conditions:

1. The person pictured in both the top and bottom rows was not wearing a hat and/or the same top in both photographs, but the different person was dressed to match the photograph on top (i.e., the paraphernalia was set up to fool the participants). However, all three pictures portrayed the same facial expression.

2. The paraphernalia were set up to trick the participants, as in Condition 1. However, the person that was in both the top and bottom rows had the same facial expression in both her photographs, but the different person did not have the same expression (i.e., the facial expression was set up to be helpful).

3. All three photographs depicted the same paraphernalia, but the person's facial expression in the top row matched a different person's facial expression on the bottom (i.e., the facial expression was set up to trick the participants).

4. The paraphernalia were set up to match the same person on the top and bottom rows, but the facial expressions did not match (i.e., set up to trick for expression but to help for paraphernalia).

Diamond and Carey (1977) found that for 6-year-olds, there were significant differences between all conditions, with Condition 1 being the hardest, Condition 2 the second hardest, Condition 3 the third hardest, and Condition 4 the easiest. For 8-year-olds, Conditions 1, 2, and 3 and 4 still differed significantly in terms of difficulty, but Conditions 3 and 4 were comparable to each other. At age 10, the only difference was between Condition 1 and the other three conditions. The expression changes were never more difficult than the paraphernalia changes. Diamond and Carey concluded that children appear to rely on isolated features to make identifications.

When Freire and Lee (2001) examined the facial recognition abilities of children ages 4 to 7 using both paraphernalia changes (in the form of a hat) as well as featural and configural information changes, they found that the majority of the children used both configural and featural information to make their identifications. However, they found that when a hat was added, children who had become adept through practice at recognizing the target still had difficulty; their memories appeared to be easily disrupted by the presence of the hat in the photographs.

To examine the differences in facial perception abilities between children and adults, de Heering, Rossion, and Maurer (2012) studied children ages 6 to 12 as well as adults (M_{age} = 19 years) using the Benton Face Recognition Test, which is a tool designed for facial perception assessment.

In Part 1 of the study, participants were asked to as quickly as possible match faces presented one at a time at the top of a computer screen to a group of six smaller faces presented at the same time at the bottom of the screen. In Part 2, they were asked to match the faces to three faces out of six presented at different angles at the bottom. Half the time throughout both parts of the experiment, the faces were inverted, and the other half of the time they were upright.

In Part 1, participants of all ages matched more quickly and accurately when the faces were upright than when they were inverted (de Heering et al., 2012). However, the accuracy rates were so high that there was evidence of a ceiling effect or close-to-ceiling effect in all cases. In Part 2, all age groups performed at above chance level. Overall, upright faces were processed more accurately and more quickly than inverted faces. When shown upright faces, children ages 6 to 8 were less accurate than children ages 8 to 10. The children 10 to 12½ years old were less accurate than the adults. However, when shown inverted faces, these same comparisons revealed no significant differences. For response times, there was no interaction between age and orientation; all age groups responded more quickly to upright faces. Overall, the children from 6 to 12 years of age were equivalent, but adults were significantly faster than the children when it came to speed of processing the faces. From the ages of 8 and 12, there was evidence of similar improvement for recognition of both upright and inverted faces; this might be due to improving general cognitive processes. Some research has suggested that by the age of 5, the ability to process faces holistically has developed fully (Crookes & McKone, 2009).

How do these results apply to identification by the young eyewitness? With a target-present lineup, a gross discrimination based on features (e.g., featural processing of hair color and shape) may be sufficient to produce a correct identification (e.g., the lineup member with the hairstyle similar to the witness's memory of it may be the guilty party). With a target-absent lineup, holistic processing is necessary for identification accuracy (i.e., correct rejection). Even if there is a lineup member with a hairstyle similar to the witness's memory of it, he or she is not the guilty party, and other information must be used to reach a correct decision. If young eyewitnesses do not have access to or are not using holistic information to make identification decisions with target-absent lineups in particular, more incorrect identification decisions may be made compared with adults. Perhaps understanding differences in identification decisions between children and adults requires a consideration of the social context in which a lineup occurs.

Social Factors

It is important to keep in mind that the lineup is not just a memory task; rather, it occurs within a social context. Beal, Schmitt, and Dekle (1995) suggested that errors in identification may be due not only to memory fallibility but also to social factors. It is possible that social factors may influence children's responding to a greater degree than adults. The mere presentation of a lineup may exert an implicit demand to select someone (Ceci, Ross, & Toglia, 1987). Consider why a lineup would be shown if not to have someone selected. Children may be more susceptible than adults to adults' questions (as we saw in Chapter 3, younger children are more suggestible than older children or adults, and older children are more suggestible than adults). The young eyewitness may provide the answer he or she thinks the experimenter or police officer wants. Once an adult asks whether the target is among the photographs shown, the child may infer that the task is to select a photograph. Wells and Luus (1990) likened the lineup task to a social psychology experiment. Just as there are social demands that are experienced by the participant in an experimental task, so too does the witness experience similar demands when examining a lineup.

The mere presentation of a lineup suggests to the witness that he or she is to make a selection. Making no selection (or rejecting the lineup) may be viewed as a "nonresponse" and a participant or witness who is not willing to complete the task. For example, both participant and witness may want to please the experimenter or police officer by choosing the "right person." The participant may guess at the experimenter's hypothesis. The witness may guess whom the police suspect and whom the officer wants the witness to choose. Moreover, the social demands associated with a lineup task may be more pronounced for the younger eyewitness. For example, the experimenter or police officer is an authority figure who is older than the child. There is an implicit demand to make a selection when shown a lineup: Why would you be shown a lineup if not to pick someone out? The young eyewitness may worry about getting into trouble if no selection is made because this behavior would suggest noncompliance. For example, Pozzulo and Lindsay (1997) found that children were less likely to use an "I don't know" response than were adults, even when this response option was made salient. Thus, children's higher false positive rates compared with adults' may occur because of a greater sense of the need to make a selection or identification when shown a lineup (e.g., J. F. Parker & Ryan, 1993; Pozzulo & Lindsay, 1998).

Steblay (1997) described two types of social influence: normative and informational. *Normative* social influence relates to wanting to gain approval and not obtain disapproval. *Informational* social influence occurs when accepting information from others as the truth. Both types of social influence may be operating on children to a greater degree than adults. Although referring to adult eyewitnesses, Steblay suggested that when a witness is shown a lineup by an authority figure, both normative and informational social influence might be operational. The assumption is that if the target is in the lineup, the correct decision is to make a selection.

To tackle the aspect of the influence of an authority figure on children's identification accuracy, Lowenstein, Blank, and Sauer (2010) had 9- and 10-year-olds view a staged crime and later identify a burglar from a (simultaneous—all lineup members shown at the same time) lineup that was either target-present or target-absent. The lineup administrator was either wearing a uniform or not. As Lowenstein et al. pointed out, a lineup administrator wearing a uniform may "increase both informational influence (as the lineup administrator will be perceived as more credible) and normative influence (because the lineup administrator will be perceived as an important source of approval or disapproval)" (p. 61). Status and authority would be predicted to heighten the problems with children's identification decisions. Indeed, children in the uniform-present condition made significantly more choices than children in the non-uniform conditions. In the uniform condition, children made more false positive identifications (target-absent lineup) than when a uniform was not present. Lowenstein et al. found that their pattern of results indicated that in the presence of someone wearing a uniform, children want to comply and appear competent, which may override their memory for the target.

Further evidence for children perceiving a greater demand to select someone from a lineup compared with adults is obtained by examining the types of errors children make on target-present lineups compared with adults. On the basis of the foil identification data available from the studies in the Pozzulo and Lindsay (1998) meta-analysis, the rate of foil identification made by older children versus adults given a target-present lineup was examined. Across six hypothesis tests, older children made significantly more foil identifications (.34) than adults (.11). We should interpret this cautiously, however, given the small sample. If we consider the target-absent lineup conditions, an analysis of nine different comparisons between children's and adults' false positive identification rates (see Dekle, Beal, Elliott, & Huneycutt, 1996; Lindsay, Pozzulo, Craig, Lee, & Corber, 1997; J. F. Parker & Ryan, 1993; Pozzulo & Balfour, 2006; Pozzulo & Dempsey, 2006) indicated that children made significantly more false positive identifications (.72) compared with adults (.39). Children do seem to guess or pick more often than adults.

Although adults too may perceive pressure to make an identification, children are likely to perceive greater pressure than adults. For example, using both a child and adult sample, Pozzulo and Dempsey (2006) found that with biased lineup instructions (i.e., instructions that do not explicitly state an option to reject the lineup), children had a higher rate of false positives compared with adults. In the same study, children also had a higher rate of false positive responding compared with adults when neutral or nonbiased lineup instructions were presented. Thus, the researchers found that a manipulation known to increase false positives in adults (i.e., lineup instructions; Malpass & Devine, 1981; Steblay, 1997) also increased false positives in children. Moreover, the proportional increase in false positive responding between children and adults remained constant across neutral and biased instructions.

In contrast, correct identification rates seem unaffected by pressure (e.g., Malpass & Devine, 1981). Correct rejection rates (target-present lineups) are influenced when the child feels pressure to make a selection but does not see the target, so another individual is selected. If children's false positive responding with target-absent lineups is driven by social demands of the task to a greater degree than cognitive demands (i.e., memory), even with a lower cognitive demand lineup task (i.e., familiar target), children should produce a higher false positive rate than adults. A caveat is necessary at this point: I am not suggesting that eyewitness identification can be neatly split into two crude categories of "social" and "cognitive." Certainly, identification involves both social and cognitive processes, and this interplay varies depending on the factors present at the time of encoding, the individual eyewitness, and so forth. Rather, I have used the terms *social* and *cognitive* as labels for groups of factors and processes where one group of factors and processes may be more prevalent under certain conditions.

Pozzulo, Dempsey, Bruer, and Sheahan (2012) defined a lower cognitive demand lineup task as one in which the correct identification rate would be 100%. In such a case, false positives would have to be driven by social factors to a greater degree than cognitive factors; that is, accurate identification is at ceiling with the target-present lineup, so an error in the target-absent lineup must be a result of social pressure more so than cognitive factors. Using a within-subjects design would eliminate the possibility of explaining the results as a function of individual differences. It was predicted that young children and adults would produce comparable correct identification rates (with a lower cognitive demand lineup). Assuming that errors (i.e., false positive responding) are driven by social factors more so than cognitive factors in the target-absent condition, it was predicted that young children would produce a higher false positive rate than adults, regardless of the cognitive demand of the lineup task.

Pozzulo et al. (2012) used popular cartoon characters (i.e., *Dora the Explorer* and *Go, Diego, Go!*) and two clips of human actors engaged in everyday tasks (a female combing her hair, and a male putting on his coat). In this study, children could correctly identify the cartoon characters at approximately 100%. This indicates that the cartoon characters are familiar targets and that identifying them is a relatively easy (i.e., lower) cognitive task. If children produce near perfect correct identification rates but go on to produce significantly lower correct rejection rates (target-absent lineups) than adults, these data would provide strong support that social demands to make a selection drives children's higher false positive rate compared with adults. Pozzulo et al. (2012) felt it important to compare within the same study and across the same participants the identification patterns using human faces as well as cartoon faces. Using human face stimuli provides a baseline of sorts to understand better the influence of unfamiliar (i.e., human faces) versus familiar (i.e., cartoon faces) stimuli. Moreover, these data could be compared with data from other studies that use human face stimuli. Young children (4–7 years old) and adults were shown a series of targets that were either familiar (i.e., popular cartoon characters) or unfamiliar (unknown human faces) to assess whether children's false positive responding with target-absent lineups is driven by social factors to a greater degree than cognitive factors. Although children were able to produce correct identification rates with virtually 100% accuracy for the cartoon characters, they produced a significantly lower correct rejection rate compared with adults. In comparison with adults, children also produced a significantly lower correct rejection rate for the human faces. Even with targets they can easily identify, children go on to make errors when shown a lineup and these targets are not present.

The data by Pozzulo et al. (2012) are intriguing, in particular with regard to the cartoon faces where, given the high rates of correct identification, the children clearly knew the characters and could identify them. However, in the target-absent cartoon conditions, 20% to 33% of children were making an erroneous selection when asked to pick out Dora or Diego from the photo arrays. Thus, some factor or set of factors seemed to compel children to make a selection rather than a rejection.

Decision Criterion

J. F. Parker and Carranza (1989) suggested that the children may be using a lower decision criterion than adults to make a selection. This notion may be connected to the demand characteristics of feeling as if you have to make a selection. Given this expectation that children have to make a selection from a lineup, they may be reducing the degree to which there has to be a match between their memory for the target and the faces presented. Even a somewhat loose match to the child's memory may be sufficient for an identification to be made. Adults may have a higher criterion for a match before they make an identification, even when feeling a sense of expectation to make a selection.

Type of Decision

The actual response of an identification versus a rejection differs. With an identification, one is making a selection, whereas with a rejection, one is not making a selection per se (note that this notion is part of the rationale for providing children with an outlined silhouette as part of a lineup). An identification involves recognizing a previously seen face (i.e., a recognition task), whereas a rejection involves recalling a face and determining that the face is not present in the lineup (i.e., recall task). Making an identification is considered a positive response, whereas a rejection is considered a negative response. It has been suggested that children view giving positive responses as being more favorable than giving negative responses (Zajac & Karageorge, 2009); this is to say that children prefer making an identification rather than rejecting a lineup.

Malpass and Devine (1981) found that adults making an identification choice (i.e., positive response) had a higher confidence score, whereas those asked to reject a lineup had a lower confidence score, possibly suggesting that adults also view giving positive responses as being more favorable than giving negative responses. Moreover, participants in the identification condition (i.e., asked to make a choice or positive response) showed confidence levels nearly five times higher than those who did not choose (i.e., displayed a negative response). Sporer, Penrod, Read, and

Cutler (1995) conducted a meta-analysis and found that the mean confidence-accuracy level for correct choosers (those making identifications, positive responses) was consistently higher than for nonchoosers (those participants rejecting lineups; providing negative responses). It is possible that not choosing produces a lack of sureness in the witness. Adults may be better able to overcome this than can young eyewitnesses.

CONCLUSION

Explanations for differences in recall and recognition between young and adult eyewitness are somewhat similar, in that both recall and recognition involve memory and can be influenced by the social context. However, there also are nuanced differences, given that recall and recognition are different types of memory tasks and that social context may exert different influences. The following chapter explores the relation between recall and recognition. Does the performance on one task tell us anything about the performance on the other? Ultimately, the way forward to improving evidence from the young eyewitness may be to apply our understanding of the differences between children and adults to the procedures we use both for recall and recognition.

7

Relation Between Describing the Perpetrator and Identifying the Perpetrator

As discussed in Chapter 2, children and adult eyewitnesses alike provide few descriptors, and those descriptors can apply to many individuals. Young eyewitnesses, however, tend to provide even fewer descriptors than did adults. For example, it is not uncommon for young children of 4 and 5 years of age to provide two or three descriptors. More information may be obtained by further questioning; however, the nature of the questioning is critical to maximizing the likelihood that the information obtained is accurate. It is possible that even with further questioning, little information is reported. It can be assumed that witnesses who report few descriptors may have a poor memory of the perpetrator and may not be able to correctly identify the perpetrator. However, is such an assumption valid? With young eyewitnesses more likely than adults to report fewer descriptors, is their ability to make an accurate identification decision

http://dx.doi.org/10.1037/14956-008
The Young Eyewitness: How Well Do Children and Adolescents Describe and Identify Perpetrators?
by J. Pozzulo

viewed more skeptically? Does the connection exist between recalling what a perpetrator looks like and accurately identifying him or her? Are poorer descriptions with few items or descriptions with inaccurate items more likely to be associated with inaccurate identification decisions, and does this hold for the young (and adult) eyewitness? Few studies have been conducted with these questions specifically in mind. Thus, definitive conclusions should be tentative. Suggestions follow as to why describing a stranger and then identifying him or her may not be particularly related. A synopsis of the studies on the topic is provided to give the reader a sense of the studies that have been conducted and what has been found. More work has to be done to examine hypotheses on the relation between describing and identifying across ages to gain a fuller understanding of the phenomenon.

WHY DESCRIBING AND IDENTIFYING MAY NOT BE RELATED

After a description is provided, witnesses may also be asked to identify a perpetrator. Providing a description is a recall task that is dependent on verbal ability, whereas identification is a recognition task almost independent of linguistic demands (other than being able to understand the task instructions). Recall and recognition tasks may be driven by different processes (Wells, 1984). Ellis (1984) suggested that verbal processes may be irrelevant to encoding and recognizing faces (see also Chance & Goldstein, 1976; Goldstein, Johnson, & Chance, 1979; Malpass, Lavigueur, & Weldon, 1973). Retrieval cues for recall tasks may differ from those for recognition tasks (Flexser & Tulving, 1978). In addition, a significant relation has not been found between description accuracy and identification accuracy for adults (Cutler, Penrod, & Martens, 1987; Pigott & Brigham, 1985; Pigott, Brigham, & Bothwell, 1990). However, Sporer (1996) reported a significant relationship between description length (number of descriptors) and correct identification decisions for adults. Witnesses who made a correct decision reported more descriptors ($M = 6.52$ descriptors) than witnesses who made an incorrect decision ($M = 5.16$ descriptors).

WHAT DOES THE DESCRIPTION–IDENTIFICATION RELATION LOOK LIKE FOR THE YOUNG EYEWITNESS?

In a study with children and adults, Pozzulo and Warren (2003) examined the relation between age, description quantity, and identification accuracy (you can read more about this study in Chapter 2). When examining target-present lineups, the number of descriptors reported by 10- to 14-year-olds did not vary across identification accuracy (correct identification vs. inaccurate decision). Also, the number of descriptors did not vary for adults across identification accuracy. This pattern of results also held for target-absent lineups. Specifically, 10- to 14-year-olds also reported a similar number of descriptors when making a correct rejection versus a false positive identification. Also, adults reported a similar number of descriptors when making a correct rejection versus a false positive identification. Ten- to 14-year-olds reported significantly fewer descriptors ($M = 7.75$ descriptors) than did adults ($M = 9.65$ descriptors) when making a correct rejection, as well as fewer descriptors ($M = 7.20$ descriptors) than did adults ($M = 12.00$ descriptors) when making a false positive identification. In Study 2, Pozzulo and Warren (2003) examined target-present lineups and found that the number of descriptors did not vary for young eyewitnesses across identification accuracy (correct identification vs. inaccurate decision). Also, the number of descriptors did not vary for adult eyewitnesses across identification accuracy (correct identification vs. inaccurate decision). For target-absent lineups, the results replicated those in Study 1.

Description length may be used inappropriately to assess a witness's memory and ability to make accurate lineup decisions. Young eyewitnesses provided fewer descriptors than did adults, regardless of identification accuracy. The young participants reported a similar number of descriptors, whether they were accurate or inaccurate. The same pattern was present for adults. There does appear to be a bigger gap between young eyewitnesses and adults regarding the number of descriptors reported for target-absent lineups and identification accuracy decisions. That is, there appears to be a larger gap in descriptors as a function of age when making a false positive identification versus correct rejection. Again, it is not clear what we should make of this finding. We saw in Chapters 4 and 5 that young eyewitnesses, compared with adults, have difficulty correctly rejecting target-absent lineups. These young eyewitnesses may also provide a briefer description, possibly due to poorer memory or being more suggestible. However, adults outperform children in terms of correct identifications as well (Fitzgerald & Price, 2015). Thus, the descriptor and identification relation have to be better teased apart. More research is needed to understand better this relation and to determine whether it is stable and, if so, why it occurs.

In another set of studies with a somewhat younger set of young eyewitnesses, Pozzulo, Dempsey, Crescini, and Lemieux (2009) examined the relationship between eyewitness recall of a perpetrator and identification of the perpetrator. Children (M_{age} = 10.25 years) and young adults (M_{age} = 21.73 years) were shown a videotaped theft of a purse in a university laboratory. Participants were then asked to write down everything they could remember about the crime and the perpetrator's appearance. After completing the descriptions, participants were presented with a six-person simultaneous lineup. Descriptions were coded for the total number of descriptors given and the proportion of correct descriptors. Although children reported fewer event details and fewer person descriptors than adults, there was no relationship between number of descriptors recalled and identification accuracy for both children and adults (Pozzulo, Dempsey, Crescini, et al., 2009). Similarly, no relationship was found for recall accuracy and identification accuracy, nor were there any age differences. See Table 7.1 for the mean total of crime details and criminal descriptors as a function of age and lineup accuracy for target-absent lineups.

A second study was conducted using different stimuli to examine the robustness of these results and to increase generalizability. In addition to using a target-absent lineup, a target-present lineup was included. Only one lineup was presented to each participant. In Study 2, Pozzulo, Dempsey, Crescini, et al. (2009) had children (M_{age} = 10.35 years, age range 9–12 years) and adults (M_{age} 20.92 years, age range 18–47 years) watch a staged theft in a food court of a local shopping mall. Children and adults had a comparable

Table 7.1

Mean Total Crime Details and Criminal Descriptors as a Function of Age and Lineup Accuracy for Target-Absent Lineups

	Identification accuracy	
	Correct rejection (*n*)	Incorrect selection (*n*)
Event details		
Child	7.90 descriptors (21)	6.59 descriptors (19)
Adult	9.81 descriptors (16)	10.14 descriptors (14)
Person details		
Child	6.81 descriptors (21)	6.53 descriptors (19)
Adult	11.06 descriptors (16)	9.36 descriptors (14)

Note. From Study 1 in "Examining the Relation Between Eyewitness Recall and Recognition for Children and Adults," by J. D. Pozzulo, J. L. Dempsey, C. Crescini, and J. M. T. Lemieux, 2009, *Psychology, Crime & Law, 15*, p. 416. Copyright 2009 by Taylor & Francis. Adapted with permission.

correct identification rate and a lower correct rejection rate. When asked to describe both the event and the target, children reported significantly fewer descriptors than adults. Children were not less accurate when describing the event or target compared with adults, however. Moreover, witnesses who made an accurate lineup decision did not recall more event details or target descriptors than witnesses who made an inaccurate lineup decision. This pattern was true for both children and adults. As well, witnesses (children or adults) who made an accurate identification decision did not recall more accurate event or target details than witnesses who made an inaccurate identification decision. Although children provided fewer descriptors than adults, neither children nor adults who correctly identified the target or correctly rejected the lineup provided more descriptors. Moreover, children and adults who made a correct identification or correct rejection had recall that was just as accurate as witnesses who made an identification error. In both studies, the data did not support a positive relation between identification and recall for child and/or adult witnesses. Thus, little can be inferred about a witness's identification accuracy from their recall. For young eyewitnesses, these data are particularly significant, given children's tendency to provide briefer descriptions of the event and person witnessed.

Witnesses making a known identification error (i.e., a foil identification) should not necessarily have their testimony for the crime and the criminal description ignored. This is an issue of critical importance for children, given their propensity to make false positive identifications. Both child and adult witnesses' reliability for recall appears to be independent of their reliability for recognition.

Results from a different study with slightly younger young eyewitnesses seem to be consistent with these studies. Specifically, Memon and Rose (2002) examined whether obtaining a verbal description of the perpetrator hinders identification accuracy. Children (M_{age} = 8.42 years) saw a stranger who had lost his dog near the school. He walked in front of each child and showed him or her a picture of this dog. After a 24-hour delay, participants in the description group were asked for a free recall description of the stranger and were also given a verbal description checklist in which they were asked specific questions about the physical features of the stranger. Participants in the control group were asked to complete a reading comprehension test in place of the recall questions. Next, participants were presented with a six-person simultaneous lineup. No relation was found between correct face descriptions and performance on the identification task.

Similarly, Zajac and Karageorge (2009) examined the relationship between description and identification with children (M_{age} = 10.03). The children went to a police station where they were given a presentation on the role of a police officer. Halfway through the presentation, a confederate came in asking to borrow a set of keys. The police officer then handed the keys to the confederate, stating he was too busy to show him which key was the right key. The confederate then left the room. Children were interviewed 1 day after the visit to the police station; those who remembered that a man came to borrow keys were then asked for a verbal description of him and were presented with a six-person simultaneous or wild card lineup. Children's accuracy in their verbal description of the confederate was unrelated to lineup accuracy (Zajac & Karageorge, 2009).

In a follow-up study, Karageorge and Zajac (2011) examined the description–identification relationship with younger children (M_{age} = 5.71 years) and older children (M_{age} = 9.19 years). A similar procedure to that of Zajac and Karageorge (2009) was used, except this time children went to a fire station. Children were then interviewed after a 1- to 2-day delay or a 2-week delay about what they could remember about the confederate who interrupted the firefighter, and they were then presented with a simultaneous or wild card lineup. Younger children gave fewer descriptors than older children when the interview was conducted 2 weeks later. Overall, older children provided more accurate descriptors than younger children. However, neither the number of descriptors reported nor the accuracy of descriptors reported were significantly related to lineup accuracy for either age group. These findings are similar to those in Zajac and Karageorge.

An adult or child witness's description of the perpetrator cannot tell you much about whether the identification made by the witness is accurate. Consider a study that focused exclusively on adult participants, Pozzulo, Dempsey, O'Neill, and Grech (2009) examined the relationship between an eyewitness's (M_{age} = 20.00 years) recall of a perpetrator and the identification of the perpetrator. Participants were shown a videotaped theft in a CD store. A woman was shown browsing in a CD store, after which she left the store with three CDs without paying for them. After viewing the video, participants were asked to write down everything they could remember about the perpetrator. After a 5- to 7-day delay, participants were then presented with a six-person simultaneous lineup. Participants' descriptions of the perpetrator were examined for the total number of descriptors given and the proportion of correct descriptors. Pozzulo, Dempsey, O'Neill, et al. found that there was no relationship between identification accuracy and total number of descriptors reported, proportion of accurate descriptors reported, or type of descriptor errors reported. Participants who made a correct identification decision provided comparable rates of total descriptors, accurate descriptors, and type of descriptor errors compared with those who made an incorrect identification decision. Pozzulo, Dempsey, O'Neill, et al. then examined whether there was a relationship between identification accuracy and descriptor category. Three descriptor categories were created: total face, total body, and total clothing. When examining whether identification accuracy was associated with the quantity of descriptors for each category, no relationship was found; participants who made a correct identification decision did not recall perpetrator details for a particular category more accurately than those who made an incorrect identification decision.

WHAT DO THESE RESULTS MEAN FOR THE REAL WORLD?

The U.S. Supreme Court ruling in *Neil v. Biggers* (1972) outlined five criteria that should be used in evaluating eyewitness identification. The criteria included the quality of the view of the perpetrator, the amount of attention paid to the perpetrator, the eyewitness's confidence, the amount of time between the crime and the identification, and the accuracy of the witness's description of the perpetrator. The last criterion is particularly relevant to this chapter. Although the U.S. Supreme Court provided these criteria, the research to date does not necessarily support the link between a witness's description and identification of a perpetrator. According to the information we currently have, which is limited in a number of ways (e.g., methodological, diversity), there does not appear to be a relation between description length or accuracy and identification accuracy. Again, only a few studies have examined this relation for the young eyewitness, so conclusions should remain tentative. If there were a relation, what would it mean? Although a police officer may have a sense that the eyewitness has provided several details (remember the description provided by the 16-year-old eyewitness in Chapter 2), there is no consensus on what constitutes a "long" versus a "short" description. Are five descriptors a short description or a long description? If description length was related to identification accuracy, how would one determine what makes a shorter versus longer description? Would description length vary depending on type of crime or other factors?

Also, in real-life cases, police do not know whether a witness, whether a child or adult, has reported accurate or inaccurate descriptors. There is no answer key for police to score witnesses' descriptions—things certainly would be easier if there were. It is reasonable to presume that descriptions may contain some accurate and some inaccurate information, but how many inaccuracies must there be before we determine that a description is inaccurate? Are one or two mistakes few enough that a description would still be considered accurate? It appears that making inferences about recall from recognition accuracy is not prudent for young (or adult) eyewitnesses at this time, from a real-world perspective.

CONCLUSION

In real-world lineups in which the perpetrator is not known, there is no way to assess a witness's description for accuracy. Keep in mind that police do not know whether they are showing a witness a target-present or target-absent lineup because the objective of showing a lineup is to determine whether the suspect is or is not guilty. Thus, research that finds tenuous relations between descriptions and a particular type of lineup (present or absent) does not appear to have a real-world application or value. If a young eyewitness provides a few descriptors, it does not suggest that their accuracy with lineup identification will be any worse or better than a young eyewitness who provides a longer description. Consider two witnesses to the same crime: One witness recalls five descriptors to describe the perpetrator and the other witness recalls 10 items. The limited data at present do not suggest that the identification decisions of either of these witnesses should have greater value or be perceived as more accurate. Much more research in this area would be useful, given the limited number of studies available from which to draw conclusions. Thus, I remain cautious about these conclusions.

8

Jurors' Perceptions of
the Young Eyewitness

In previous chapters we explored the ability of the young eyewitness to provide descriptions and identifications of a stranger–perpetrator. We examined protocols and procedures as well as other factors that may influence the young eyewitness. Once this evidence is obtained, it may make its way to the courtroom, where the young eyewitness will testify. This chapter examines the juror–jury decision-making research available on young eyewitnesses giving testimony.[1] A distinction has to be made between the eyewitness who is a bystander versus the eyewitness who is a victim. Much of the jury–juror decision-making research has been conducted with the child as eyewitness–victim, where the crime was child sexual abuse. In these cases and studies, the identity of the perpetrator

---

[1] The majority of research in this area has focused on individuals acting as jurors making individual decisions, hence the term *juror decision making*. Far less work has examined the perceptions of groups as it relates to the young eyewitness. Thus, the research reviewed in this chapter examines juror decision-making literature for the most part; however, jury decision-making research is provided when available and relevant.

http://dx.doi.org/10.1037/14956-009
The Young Eyewitness: How Well Do Children and Adolescents Describe and Identify Perpetrators?
by J. Pozzulo
Copyright © 2017 by the American Psychological Association. All rights reserved.

may not be an issue. Thus, the literature describing the young eyewitness–victim of child sexual abuse may not apply to cases in which the young eyewitness is an eyewitness–bystander and is providing a description of the perpetrator and making a lineup identification. In this chapter, I provide an overview of the perceptions of the young eyewitness–bystander and the young eyewitness–victim, where the literature permits. Comparisons with adult witnesses will be made when possible as well.

In cases that lead to prosecution, eyewitnesses (young and old) may be called to take the stand and provide critical testimony, often describing what and who was seen, as well as providing an identification (typically, prior identification would have occurred where the eyewitness identified the suspect, who is now the defendant). The eyewitness may also be asked to make an in-court identification (i.e., "Do you see the accused in the courtroom?"). The eyewitness then may identify the defendant as the perpetrator. Eyewitnesses who take the stand may play a pivotal role in the prosecution and conviction of the defendant. Cases may be tried by judge alone or by jury. Jury (and juror) decision-making research has spanned over 100 years and will not be reviewed comprehensively here. There are several good sources for a broader perspective of jury–juror decision-making (e.g., Bornstein & Greene, 2011; Devine, 2012). Here, I focus on the young eyewitness who takes the stand and on the factors that may influence jurors' perceptions and perhaps ultimately the verdict.

EYEWITNESS AGE

Understanding the perceptions of a young eyewitness are more complicated than just examining the age of the eyewitness. However, I begin by reviewing the literature on eyewitness age generally and then move to consider other factors that may interact with age of eyewitness to influence jurors' perceptions. Generally, researchers have found that adults perceive young eyewitnesses as having less accurate memories than do adults (Bottoms & Goodman, 1994; Goodman, Golding, Helgeson, Haith, & Michelli, 1987; Ross, Dunning, Toglia, & Ceci, 1990; Ross, Jurden, Lindsay, & Keeney, 2003). However, children also are perceived as honest

(Nuñez, Kehn, & Wright, 2011; Ross et al., 1990, 2003). The age of the young eyewitness can influence those perceptions, however.

D. B. Wright, Hanoteau, Parkinson, and Tatham (2010) examined the relation between age and perceived memory factors. Participants considered children between the ages of 3 and 18 and rated their perceptions of reliability and honesty for one of two events. The first event took place in the child's home where he or she was witness to her parents arguing and the alleged physical abuse of the mother. The second event took place at the child's school where he or she was witness to alleged sexual abuse by a teacher of another student in a classroom. Participants were then asked how reliable and honest they perceived the witness to be. Participants believed that memory reliability increased with witness age (D. B. Wright et al., 2010). Perceived reliability was found to increase substantially between age 3 and 6; however, once a child reached age 6, the increase was small and variable. Participants thought that honesty increased for both boys and girls until they were 5 to 6 years old, after which honesty ratings of girls continued to increase, whereas boys were perceived as less likely to be telling the truth. These upward gender trends continued until witnesses were 18 years old.

How are jurors' perceptions affected when chronological age differs from developmental age? Peled, Iarocci, and Connolly (2004) looked at how young eyewitnesses with a mild intellectual disability were perceived in terms of credibility. Participants read eyewitness testimony that varied the eyewitness's chronological age and mental age. Half the participants read about an eyewitness with a chronological age of 15 years and a mental age of 10 years. The other half read about an eyewitness who was developing normally for a 15-year-old or 10-year-old. The eyewitness with a mental age of 10 years was perceived as less credible than a typically developing 15-year-old or a typically developing 10-year-old. However, when participants responded to specific questions about the eyewitness, no significant differences emerged.

Perhaps the best way to summarize the influence of age of eyewitness on jurors' perceptions is to say that, at times, older children are perceived as more credible, and at other times, younger children are perceived as more credible. Gender may or may not have an influence on the age at which credibility increases or decreases. A variety of factors, including type of crime, may be relevant in understanding jurors' perceptions. Next, I review some of these factors as well as a model of credibility for young eyewitnesses.

UNDERSTANDING THE FACTORS THAT MAY INFLUENCE HOW THE YOUNG EYEWITNESS IS PERCEIVED

Early research examining mock jurors' perceptions of child witnesses suggested that two underlying principles influence how jurors perceive the young eyewitness. Goodman, Bottoms, Herscovici, and Shaver (1989) suggested that the first principle is that jurors may believe that children are as honest as adults, and that may lead them to believe child witnesses. The second principle they proposed is that jurors may believe that children's cognitive abilities are less developed than adults', and that may lead jurors to question a child witness's testimony (see also Goodman, Golding, & Haith, 1984). In general, younger children are viewed as more honest than older children; however, older children are viewed as more cognitively competent than younger children.

As mentioned earlier, the young eyewitness taking the stand can either be an eyewitness or an eyewitness as well as a victim. Perceptions of a young eyewitness or young eyewitness–victim may differ, and it is not surprising that we often assume a young eyewitness–victim is a victim of child abuse and, more specifically, child sexual abuse. Bottoms, Golding, Stevenson, Wiley, and Yozwiak (2007) noted that the majority of cases that make their way to the courtroom involving the young eyewitness are child sexual abuse cases. However, of course, there are numerous real-life cases of horrific child physical abuse and neglect. In actuality, only 9% of substantiated child maltreatment cases are sexual abuse cases (U.S. Department of Health & Human Services, 2013). Sexual abuse cases may lack physical evidence or additional witnesses and may rely to a greater extent on the testimony of the young eyewitness than other types of cases.

In child sexual abuse (CSA) cases, younger children may be perceived as more credible because jurors may believe they are more honest and lack the knowledge and cognitive abilities to fabricate sexual claims (Bottoms, 1993). In cases not involving CSA, older children may be viewed as more credible. For example, Goodman et al. (1987) examined mock jurors' perceived credibility of child witnesses in a vehicular homicide versus murder case; mock jurors rated the 6-year-old witness as less credible than the 30-year-old witness in both these cases. These studies suggest that a child witness's perceived credibility may depend on the type of case and whether honesty or cognitive competency is more important.

A useful model proposed by Ross et al. (2003) describes how jurors may perceive child witnesses. Ross et al. (2003) referred to this as the two-factor model of child witness credibility and suggested that it can aid in understanding how jurors perceive the young eyewitness. On the basis of previous research (e.g., Goodman et al., 1984, 1989; Ross et al., 1990), Ross and colleagues (2003) also proposed that a child witness's perceived credibility may be a function of two separate factors: cognitive ability and honesty. In Experiment 1, mock jurors viewed a sexual abuse trial in which the child was accusing her father of sexual abuse. Participants viewed testimony from the child, the father, and an expert witness. They were then asked to rate the child's honesty and cognitive ability on a series of dimensions and to render a verdict. Experiment 2 was identical to Experiment 1, except that only the testimony of a child witness was viewed. Results were similar for both studies. A two-factor model of child credibility emerged, with honesty and cognitive ability as two distinct factors; however, only honesty was found to predict verdict decisions. These results are similar to those from previous research that found perceived honestly may be more influential in cases involving CSA.

Some studies have found that children older than 12 are perceived as more credible than younger children (e.g., Bruer & Pozzulo, 2014). However, as we have seen, this perception can be altered when we consider the crime of sexual abuse. For example, Nightingale (1993) found that witnesses of a younger age are more credible than those of an older age; that is, as a young person's age increases, their credibility decreases. It has been suggested that because younger children are more naïve sexually than older children (e.g., adolescents), younger children are more believable in sexual abuse cases (Castelli, Goodman, & Ghetti, 2005).

Can the two-factor model be extended to include developmentally delayed adolescents? Bottoms, Nysse-Carris, Harris, and Tyda (2003) examined the influence of a developmentally delayed victim on mock jurors' decision making. Participants were presented with a written summary and videotaped testimony of a sexual abuse case involving a 16-year-old victim. The victim had either mild retardation or average intelligence. Mock jurors perceived the victim with mild retardation more favorably than the victim with average intelligence. Bottoms and colleagues found support for the two-factor model of credibility: When the victim was presented as having mild retardation, she was rated as more credible, honest, and less likely to fabricate the story. These results suggest that the two-factor model also can extend to developmentally delayed adolescent victims of sexual abuse. In fact, adolescents with developmental delays may be perceived similarly to young children without developmental delay. Mock jurors were also more likely to vote for a guilty verdict and have higher confidence in the defendant's guilt when the victim had mild retardation.

Can the two-factor model be extended to cases that do not include CSA? Nuñez et al. (2011) conducted such a study, with participants reading a summary in which the victim accused her stepfather of repeated sexual abuse over a 3-month period. In the no CSA condition, participants were told that the study focused on perceptions of children, and they were asked to think of a typical boy or girl of a particular age. Participants were then asked to answer a series of questions concerning the victim's testimony. Across conditions, victim gender was manipulated, as was victim age (i.e., 3, 5, 7, 9, 11, 13, or 15 years old). Nuñez and colleagues found that children were considered to be paying more attention and to have better memories and to be more trusting, reliable, and honest in cases involving CSA versus cases with no CSA. Mock jurors also believed that children were less reliable under the age of 8, after which reliability leveled off and became relatively stable. Overall, mock jurors believed that cognitive skills increase with age up until 7 to 10 years old; similarly, mock jurors believed honesty peaked during childhood and then started dropping in adolescence. These results suggest that type of crime may influence perceptions of the young eyewitness. To tease apart whether just being a victim or whether age is critical, studies have to examine types of crimes and age of the victim, as well as the role of the eyewitness (i.e., victim vs. bystander).

EYEWITNESS–VICTIM VERSUS EYEWITNESS–BYSTANDER

As mentioned earlier, a key variable that has been examined and been found to affect perceptions of the young eyewitness is the type of crime, namely, sexual abuse. It is important to keep in mind that in studies using sexual abuse as the type of crime to evaluate the young eyewitness's testimony, the young eyewitness is also the victim. We cannot compare studies in which the young eyewitness was a victim with studies in which the young eyewitness was a bystander. Comparing these types of studies results in a confound; that is, a study would have to compare crimes in which the role of the eyewitness was held constant. For example, in a study comparing a victim of sexual assault with a bystander to murder, the role of the eyewitness and the type of crime, is confounded. Hence, I next discuss the literature with an eye toward grouping studies that do not confound age of eyewitness, role of eyewitness, and type of crime.

Perceptions of a Young Eyewitness–Victim

Bottoms and Goodman (1994, Experiment 1) examined jurors' reactions to children's testimony concerning sexual abuse. A female student (6, 14, or 22 years old) claimed she was sexually abused by a male teacher in the school. When examining credibility judgments, the youngest victim was judged to be more credible than the adult witness. The defendant was also judged to be less credible when the victim was 6 years old rather than 22 years old. The 6-year-old victim elicited higher guilty ratings for the defendant than did the 14-year-old and 22-year-old victims. Similarly, the defendant was assigned more guilt when the victim was 6 years old rather than 22 years old.

McCauley and Parker (2001) examined whether victim age influenced jurors' judgments in a sexual abuse case. Participants read about a 6- or 13-year-old who was the victim of robbery, sexual assault by a stranger, or sexual assault by an acquaintance while walking through a park. Participants were less likely to vote guilty in the robbery case than either sexual assault case. Moreover, the victim in the robbery case was perceived as less credible than the victim in the sexual assault cases. To examine perceptions of the victim's memory and honesty, both sexual assault conditions were combined. The victim in the robbery case was perceived as being significantly less honest and having a poorer memory than the victim in the sexual assault case. The 13-year-old victim was perceived as having a better memory for the events than the 6-year-old victim; however, no effects of victim age were found to be influential in overall credibility. Although both memory and honesty predicted verdict outcome, memory was the critical predictor.

Comparing Victim and Bystander

Holcomb and Jacquin (2007) examined the influence of age and level of involvement on jurors' perceptions of a CSA case. Participants read a transcript concerning sexual abuse that manipulated witness type (victim, bystander) and age of the witness (5, 11, or 16). Mock jurors found the defendant guiltier in cases involving a bystander witness than a victim witness. There also was a trend toward an effect of witness age, with higher levels of guilt for the defendant when the witness was younger. Given that no significant effects of age were found, the older eyewitness ages (i.e., 11 and 16) were combined to create a younger witness versus older witness comparison: The younger witness elicited higher guilt ratings for the defendant than did the older witnesses.

Does a Juror's Gender Matter?

A number of studies have found that the jurors' gender does seem to influence perceptions of the young eyewitness. In CSA cases, in particular, female jurors tend to be more "pro-victim" and have a "pro-prosecution" bias compared with male jurors (Bottoms et al., 2007). Moreover, compared with male jurors, female jurors tend to believe the young eyewitness to a greater degree and are more likely to vote guilty (Bottoms et al., 2007; Quas, Bottoms, Haegerich, & Nysse-Carris, 2002). These results are not restricted to CSA cases but operate more broadly in cases involving sex crimes (e.g., Devine & Caughlin, 2014; Schutte & Hosch, 1997).

Although this juror gender effect has typically been shown when examining individual decision making, some work in small group decision making has reached similar conclusions. For example, Golding, Bradshaw, Dunlap, and Hodell (2007) varied the gender majority composition of small groups compared with an equal gender split group. Using a mock case of CSA with a 6-year-old victim, female majority groups were more likely to convict. Also intriguing was the finding that, in female majority groups, females who initially voted not guilty more often changed their final verdict than those in nonfemale majority groups.

A number of suggestions have been made to as to why women and men differ in their ratings in cases with young eyewitnesses. Bottoms (1993) speculated that women's greater likelihood of being victimized may make them more sympathetic so that they align themselves more with a young victim. Bottoms also suggested that women may be more empathic toward children than men. Gilligan (1982) suggested that the internalization of gender roles, such that women are seen as more empathic, nurturing, and caring, may influence differences in perceptions of the young victim–witness. Furthermore, Feingold (1994) suggested that women may be more nurturing than men and, hence, see their role as such, leading to a greater alliance with young victims.

AGE AND INCONSISTENT TESTIMONY

One issue that may (or may not) be more relevant for young eyewitnesses compared with older eyewitnesses or adults is the degree to which testimony contains inconsistencies or inaccuracies or simply mismatches between what was said and what was found. Consider the situation in which a perpetrator was described as having brown hair though the defendant has blonde hair. Research examining the influence of descriptor errors and testimony inconsistencies in an eyewitness's testimony has found that the presence of descriptor errors can negatively influence mock jurors' perceptions of the eyewitness (e.g., Berman, Narby, & Cutler, 1995; M. C. O'Neill & Pozzulo, 2012; Semmler & Brewer, 2002). Witnesses that make errors in their testimony are perceived less favorably than witnesses who make no errors in their testimony. Research has also found that testimony inconsistencies can elicit lower guilt ratings for a defendant (e.g., Bruer & Pozzulo, 2014; M. C. O'Neill & Pozzulo, 2012; Pozzulo & Dempsey, 2009b). The consensus is that the presence of testimonial inconsistencies can negatively influence the eyewitness's credibility.

Some studies have examined the influence of eyewitness age in conjunction with testimonial inconsistencies. Leippe and Romanczyk (1989, Experiment 3) considered the influence of eyewitness age (6, 10, or 30) and whether the testimony contained inconsistent statements. Participants read a case description involving eyewitness testimony. In relevant conditions, participants read about inconsistencies between what the eyewitness said in the courtroom testimony and police statement. Overall, participants rated the case stronger when there were no inconsistencies; similarly, the witness was rated more credible when there were no inconsistencies. Age and testimony inconsistencies also jointly influenced jurors' perceptions of witness credibility. When there were no inconsistencies in the 6-year-old witness's testimony, he was rated as significantly more credible than when there were inconsistencies in his testimony. There were no differences between consistent and inconsistent 10- and 30-year-old witnesses.

A follow-up study was conducted examining the influence of eyewitness age (6 or 30) and testimony consistency (Leippe & Romanczyk, 1989, Experiment 4). In addition, deliberating jurors were compared with individual jurors. Before deliberation, mock jurors had more favorable perceptions of the 6-year-old witness and a perceived a greater likelihood of the defendant being guilty. Once jurors had deliberated, the child witness was still viewed more favorably than the 30-year-old witness. There were no effects of testimony consistency on individual juror judgments or deliberating jurors' judgments.

More recently, Bruer and Pozzulo (2014) examined the influence on mock jurors' judgments of eyewitness age (4, 12, or 20) and number of descriptor errors made (0, 3, or 6) when recalling the perpetrator's appearance. Eyewitness age and errors had no influence on jurors' dichotomous verdicts; however, the number of errors made influenced jurors' continuous verdict ratings. Mock jurors were more likely to give higher guilt ratings when no errors were made than when six errors were made. Both age and errors were found to influence the perceptions of the eyewitness such that the 12- and 20-year-old eyewitnesses were viewed as having significantly more integrity than the 4-year-old witness. The eyewitnesses who made no descriptor errors or three descriptor errors were viewed as having significantly more integrity than the eyewitnesses who made six errors. Similarly, mock jurors rated the identification decision, perpetrator description, and event description as most reliable when zero descriptor errors were made compared with three or six errors. Eyewitness age was also influential in jurors' perceptions of the reliability of the eyewitness's description of the event; the event description was viewed as significantly more reliable when the adolescent presented the testimony than when the child witness did. Thus, inconsistency can influence perceptions and interact with age of eyewitness. The relationship is not linear, however, and one has to consider the age of the witness, the number of inconsistencies, and possibly the type of inconsistency. These factors may not necessarily influence the verdict, however.

AGE AND FAMILIARITY

To date, only one published empirical study has examined the influence of eyewitness age and familiarity with the defendant on mock jurors' decision making (Pozzulo, Pettalia, Bruer, & Javaid, 2014). However, given that the majority of crimes are committed by someone known to the victim (e.g., Miethe & Drass, 1999), it is a critical variable to consider. Flowe, Mehta, and Ebbeson (2011) reported that the defendant is familiar to the victim in approximately half of all trials. Participants read a trial transcript concerning a murder, in which the age of the witness and familiarity with the defendant were varied. Degree of familiarity was defined as seeing the defendant, the local mailman, zero, three, or six times before the crime was committed. The witness's age varied from 4, 12, or 20 years. The 20-year-old eyewitness was seen as more credible than a 4-year-old eyewitness when describing the events of the crime; similarly, the 20-year-old eye-witness was seen as more credible overall than the 4-year-old eyewitness. Familiarity with the defendant did not influence mock jurors' decisions, nor did it interact with eyewitness age. More research is needed in this critical area. Recall the case of Mary Katherine Smart, who recognized the voice of her sister's abductor (see Chapter 1). The majority of eyewitness research has focused on the stranger–perpetrator.

AGE AND SPEECH STYLE

One factor that tends to vary with age is speech style. Consider the conversation style of a 5-year-old compared with a 12-year-old compared with a 19-year-old. Individuals of these three ages would sound very different from each other. Nigro, Buckley, Hill, and Nelson (1989) examined the influence of eyewitness age and speech style on mock jurors' decision making. Participants read a trial transcript concerning a fatal car–pedestrian accident in which the eyewitness to the crime was 8 or 25 years old. The eyewitness testified in either a powerless (i.e., with hesitations while testifying) or powerful manner. Overall, mock jurors were more likely to rate the 8-year-old witness as significantly more credible than the 25-year-old witness. Mock jurors also were more likely to rate the witness who spoke powerfully as significantly more credible than the witness who spoke in a powerless manner. There was also a combined effect of eyewitness age and speech style: The 8-year-old witness who spoke in a powerful manner was viewed as most credible compared with when he or she spoke in a powerless manner.

In another study, Schmidt and Brigham (1996) examined the influence of eyewitness age and speech style; however, they also included the influence of the prosecuting attorney's questioning style. Mock jurors viewed a videotaped mock trial of a CSA case in which the age of the victim/witness was 5, 10, or 15. The witness testified in either a powerless or powerful manner. When the prosecuting attorney asked questions of the witness, the questions varied between leading and nonleading questions. Eyewitness age, speech style, and question type had no influence on verdict decisions. The 5-year-old victim was perceived as significantly more truthful and accurate than the 15-year-old victim. Both the 5- and 10-year-old victims were seen as more intelligent and self-assured than the 15-year-old victim. When the victim testified with a powerful speech style, she was viewed as more accurate and intelligent; however, this also came at a cost of mock jurors perceiving her as having suffered less from the incident and from giving testimony. Age and speech style also combined to influence mock jurors' perceived credibility of witnesses. The 15-year-old witness who spoke in a powerless manner was viewed more negatively than the other victims. The 5-year-old witness who spoke in a powerful manner was rated more positively than the victims in any other condition. The 5- and 15-year-old witnesses who spoke in a powerful manner were viewed as being more truthful and intelligent than the 5- and 15-year-old witnesses who spoke in a powerless manner. Questioning style did not have a consistent effect on perceptions of the child's credibility (Schmidt & Brigham, 1996). Age and speech style can interact; it would be interesting investigate whether type of crime is relevant.

Ruva and Bryant (2004) examined the influence of witness age, speech style, and prosecuting attorney questioning style. Participants read a trial transcript depicting a murder in which the sole eyewitness to the crime was 6, 10, or 22 years old. The witness testified in a powerless or powerful manner. Questioning from the lawyer varied between predominately open-ended questions and predominately closed-ended questions. Participants were more likely to give higher guilt ratings to the defendant when the witness was 6 years old and questioned with open-ended questions than when the 22-year-old witness was asked open-ended questions. Moreover, the 6-year-old witness who was asked closed-ended questions elicited significantly lower guilt ratings than the 10- or 22-year-old questioned the same way. The 6-year-old witness was viewed as more credible than the 22-year-old witness. Furthermore, the witness who had a powerful speech style was viewed as more credible than the witness who had a powerless speech style. As in previous studies, age and speech style combined to influence mock jurors' credibility judgments. The 22-year-old witness with a powerless speech style was perceived as significantly less credible than the 6- or 10-year-old witness with a powerless speech style. There were no differences between the 6-, 10-, or 22-year-old witnesses who spoke with a powerful speech style. Question type also combined with age to influence mock jurors, such that the 6-year-old witness who was asked predominately open-ended questions was viewed as significantly more credible than all other witnesses. A number of factors can combine and interact with the age of the eyewitness, which then may influence jurors' perceptions and possibly the verdict in some instances.

CONCLUSION

Although there is ample research examining the influence of young eyewitness characteristics on individual juror decision making, far less research has examined the influence of these characteristics on juries as a whole. Nicholson, Yarbrough, and Penrod (2014) hypothesized that the paucity of research examining the influence of these characteristics on jury deliberations may be due to the cost and time required to conduct research involving juries. Moreover, there are legal restrictions in some countries (e.g., Canada) regarding investigating the deliberation process with real-life juries Although there is limited research examining how eyewitness characteristics influence jury deliberations and decision making, previous research has confirmed that eyewitness testimony does influence jury decision making: Conviction rates rise when eyewitness testimony is introduced (e.g., Greene, 1988; Spanos, Myers, DuBreuil, & Pawlak, 1992) and even more so when the eyewitness testimony is strong and no judicial instructions are given (Greene, 1988).

Understanding how the young eyewitness is perceived when providing testimony is a complex task. As described earlier, a number of factors affect jurors' perceptions of young eyewitnesses. Not only can case factors interact with age of the eyewitness, but juror factors also play a role. For example, a juror's gender can influence their perceptions and interact with type of case (e.g., CSA), age of eyewitness, and even gender of the eyewitness. Perhaps this is the tip of the iceberg; in all likelihood, a far greater number of factors may interact with each other to influence perceptions. More research is needed to understand this complex interplay. Moreover, the type of methodology used is critical. Juror versus jury decision making that includes deliberation may produce different outcomes. Also, partial transcripts versus more complete transcripts can produce different results than a mock trial played on video. Obtaining similar results across a variety of methodologies will provide us with the most confidence that the results are stable and generalizable. For now, the majority of research we have for understanding jurors' perceptions of young eyewitnesses surrounds cases of CSA. Younger eyewitnesses can be viewed as credible and accurate in these cases as well as in cases in which they are bystanders. It is also important to keep in mind that perceptions are not verdict decisions. Again, a number of factors may interact to influence the verdict.

9

Policy Implications

The life of a young eyewitness spans a large panorama of developmental years, with numerous changes occurring throughout this time. The best practices described in this chapter are based on what we know to date for those within this broad age range. The young eyewitness, starting at about 4 years of age (we do not have sufficient research with younger young eyewitnesses), can provide accurate descriptors when describing a stranger. Anecdotally, we saw cases in Chapter 1 in which bits of descriptive information turned out to be accurate and helpful in resolving the case. There are a number of excellent interview protocols that may be helpful in increasing the information that is obtained from the young eyewitness. Those protocols are not reviewed here but rather in Chapter 3. Next, I highlight some key elements that most protocols include.

The young eyewitness, again starting at about age 4, can provide accurate identification evidence; however, this ability or performance

http://dx.doi.org/10.1037/14956-010
The Young Eyewitness: How Well Do Children and Adolescents Describe and Identify Perpetrators?
by J. Pozzulo

improves as the young eyewitness gets older. A challenge with young eye-witnesses is their difficulty in rejecting lineups that do not contain the guilty perpetrator. Of course, police do not know whether the lineup they are showing the young eyewitness contains a guilty or innocent suspect. A number of identification procedures have been developed and tested. Again, for a complete review, see Chapters 4 and 5. At present, no identi-fication procedure seems ideal for increasing the young eyewitness's abil-ity to correctly identify the perpetrator and correctly reject lineups that contain innocent suspects. Next, I describe some basic elements that may be helpful in obtaining accurate descriptive and identification evidence from young eyewitnesses.

ELICITING PERSON DESCRIPTIONS

Person descriptions are specific details about the person or persons who committed the crime. These details can be embedded in an eyewitness's account of what transpired. For example, when describing the crime, details about the perpetrator also may be elicited. Obtaining descriptions of the perpetrator should follow best practices for good interviewing. There are a number of interview protocols with best practice elements, such as the cognitive interview, step-wise interview, and the National Institute of Child Health and Human Development Interview Protocol. See Chapter 3 for a full review of these.

Common Elements of Best Practice Interview Protocols

Interview protocols that have shown success in obtaining accurate infor-mation from the young eyewitness share some common elements:

- *Rapport building.* The interviewer should talk about neutral topics with the young eyewitness to make him or her comfortable. An attempt should be made to make the young eyewitness feel comfortable with the interviewer.
- *Free recall.* Young eyewitnesses should describe what they witnessed or experienced in their own words without direct questioning or inter-

rupting. The interviewer can ask, "What did you see?" or "What did he look like?"

- *Open-ended questioning and prompts.* Young eyewitnesses may not report much information when describing the perpetrator (and/or event) using free recall; however, they may have more information to provide. The interviewer should use open-ended questioning or prompts to follow up the young eyewitness's free recall report. For example, the interviewer can say, "Tell me more" or "What happened next?" These prompts can be used more than once until it appears that the young eyewitness has no more information to provide.

- *General and nonleading questions.* The interviewer may follow up on details provided by the young eyewitness in their free recall in a manner the young eyewitness understands. For example, the interviewer may say, "Tell me more about when the teacher gets angry."

- *Conclusion.* The young eyewitness may wonder what will happen next. It is good practice to thank the young eyewitness for helping and explain what will happen next.

Elements to Avoid

There are a number of elements that many agree should be avoided to increase the likelihood of obtaining accurate information:

- Avoid incorporating misinformation into a question.
- Avoid suggesting the response desired.
- Avoid multipart questions.
- Avoid praising or scolding the young eyewitness for information they provide.
- Avoid yes/no questions, if possible.

As mentioned earlier, a number of specific interviewing protocols are available (see Chapter 3), and these elements are not intended to replace established and evaluated protocols. Rather, these elements are often shared among protocols that have had some demonstrated effectiveness. Not all interviewing protocols have been compared with each other, and as such, it is not clear whether one is more effective than all the others at eliciting complete and accurate information while limiting false information.

Elements to Consider

An interviewer may wish to consider the following elements when conducting the interview:

- Use language that the young eyewitness understands, both regarding the language spoken and the comprehension of the words chosen.
- Be aware of the young eyewitness's numeracy skills; if the child cannot count, do not ask questions that require this skill (e.g., "How many times?").
- Be aware of the young eyewitness's ability to tell time; asking about temporal elements may or may not be accurate depending on the young eyewitness's ability.
- Be aware of the young eyewitness's ability to name color (and differentiate between colors).
- Be aware of the young eyewitness's ability to name clothing items.
- Be aware of the young eyewitness's ability to name facial features.

Specific Elements in Describing a Perpetrator That May Be Helpful

Some aids may be helpful during the interview process. Note, however, that these elements have not been evaluated and should not be introduced unless the young eyewitness has (a) mentioned the item(s) and (b) does not have the developed language to describe them. Research evaluating these elements is critical before any recommendations can be made about them. Aids might include

- pictorials that help with naming items (e.g., shirts, pants, dresses),
- color swatches for hair,
- hair length and hairstyle pictorials, and
- using a reference (e.g., the interviewer) for height and weight descriptions.

OBTAINING AN IDENTIFICATION

A number of identification procedures have been developed, with some attempting to take the young eyewitness's approach to decision making into consideration. Debate continues as to which identification procedure is better at maintaining a high rate of correct identification and high correct rejection (or low false identification rate). (See Chapter 4 for a full review of the various identification procedures that have been evaluated.) Aside from the sequential lineup (in which lineup members are shown serially to the eyewitness), all other procedures seem to share a simultaneous presentation, in some way. To date, no data are available that suggest that the sequential lineup procedure is better for young eyewitnesses than others that use some sort of simultaneous format. It is possible that the sequential lineup may not be worse than the other procedures, but it is likely not better for the young eyewitness. Compared with a traditional simultaneous lineup, the elimination procedure may be more effective in increasing the rate of correct rejection for some young eyewitnesses; however, a better understanding is required of its impact on the correct identification rate.

Common Elements of Best Practice Identification Procedures

Given the data, I make only four recommendations for best practices for lineup identification by young eyewitnesses, with one cautionary note:

- Use a single-suspect model with some number of foils up to 11.
- Ensure that the suspect does not stand out compared with the other lineup members.
- Have a salient "not here" option for the young eyewitness; this option could be in the form of a silhouette.
- Inform young eyewitnesses that the criminal may or may not be present. If they see the criminal, they should pick his or her face; if they do not see the criminal, they should pick the "not here" option or silhouette.

A number of identification procedures seem to be helpful with young eyewitnesses. As with interviewing protocols, not all procedures have been compared with each other, so I am unable to recommend one procedure over the others at this time.

Reconsidering the Elimination Procedure

Not all identification procedures are created equal. It is important to consider that the elimination procedure provides additional information for the ultimate identification decision. If the elimination procedure does not decrease correct identification rates and is not worse at producing correct rejection rates than other lineup procedures, it may be worthwhile using the elimination procedure because of the additional information obtained from using this procedure. Recall that the elimination procedure (Pozzulo & Lindsay, 1999; see also Chapter 4, this volume) starts with a simultaneous presentation of lineup members and asks the eyewitness to pick out the person who looks most like the criminal. The most similar looking lineup member selected is termed the *survivor*. All the remaining lineup members are removed, and the witness is asked whether the survivor is or is not the criminal. If the survivor is not the suspect (i.e., a foil), it may suggest that the suspect is innocent. If the suspect is not picked out as the most similar looking person to the perpetrator, it is possible that the suspect is not the guilty perpetrator, assuming that a guilty suspect will look more like him- or herself than anyone else.

The elimination procedure allows police to find out whether the suspect looks the most similar to the perpetrator compared with the rest of the lineup members. If he or she does not, further investigation into other suspects might be worthwhile. No other lineup procedure to date requests an explicit decision to pick out the lineup member most similar to the perpetrator before requesting an identification decision. Of course, even if the survivor is the suspect, there is no guarantee that the suspect is guilty—hence, the essential need to ask for the identification decision. To possibly improve the elimination procedure, a silhouette could be paired with the survivor when making the identification decision to further aid eyewitnesses in their decision making. (The impact of this pairing is currently being tested to understand how correct identification and correct rejection rates are influenced.) More data are needed before any one identification procedure can be considered best practice. The elimination procedure does appear to provide information beyond the other current procedures that only request an identification decision.

A CAUTIONARY NOTE

The elimination procedure requires two judgments, whereas other procedures require one judgment, such as with the simultaneous procedure. In situations in which there are multiple suspects or in which an eyewitness is faced with having to view several lineups, the number of judgments requested quickly escalates, doubling for the elimination procedure. An adult eyewitness may be more apt at making several judgments than a 6-year-old, for example. Consider a case in which there are three lineups. Using a simultaneous procedure, the eyewitness will make three judgments, whereas using an elimination procedure six judgments are required. The number of judgments may have a negligible impact on accuracy for older young eyewitnesses or adults but perhaps not for young young eyewitnesses. This issue is an empirical question that can be tested, but at the moment it is not clear whether number of judgments affects identification accuracy as a function of age.

CONCLUSION

The criminal justice system is equipped with some knowledge of how to interview young eyewitnesses and obtain identification evidence. Although various interview protocols may be helpful in eliciting more accurate information from the young eyewitness, descriptive information about the perpetrator remains limited. Greater effort should be made at identifying tools that may aid in increasing person-description information from witnesses of all ages. A number of identification procedures are available; however, the best identification procedure to use with young eyewitnesses is unclear at this point. When different protocols and procedures for different-aged witnesses are identified as "better," it raises the question of when to switch from using one procedure to another. Ideally, if one interview protocol and one identification procedure worked with all eyewitnesses, this decision making would not be required. Should we have different procedures for different-aged witnesses, we would have to delineate when to use which procedure and under what conditions. And of course, a number of factors other than a witness's chronological age may be relevant when deciding on the protocols and procedures to use.

10

Future Directions for Young Eyewitness Research

In Chapter 1, seven cases were highlighted that involved children of various ages in an eyewitness role. Eyewitnesses are questioned for information that may lead to the apprehension of the perpetrator. The information provided by the eyewitness may also be used in the courts to determine the guilt of the defendant. When the eyewitness is a child, a number of considerations arise. The information from a young eyewitness may be viewed more cautiously, and as we have seen throughout this book, there are factors that can increase or decrease the accuracy of children's reports of the witnessed event and perpetrator and, moreover, the identification of the perpetrator. We have seen that with increasing age up to young adulthood, richer descriptions are provided and identification accuracy increases. It is important to note that no critical age has been found at which all information provided is reliable. We know that even adults may provide "thin" descriptions and inaccurate descriptions,

http://dx.doi.org/10.1037/14956-011
The Young Eyewitness: How Well Do Children and Adolescents Describe and Identify Perpetrators?
by J. Pozzulo

but we also know some factors increase the likelihood of information being more accurate, and others decrease the likelihood that the information provided is accurate. As we have seen in numerous real-life cases and laboratory studies, adult witnesses "get it wrong" sometimes, but they "get it right" sometimes as well. The same statement can be made for young eyewitnesses. Although one may conclude that children are less accurate witnesses than adults, there is ample evidence to suggest that children can provide accurate descriptive information and identifications. The young eyewitness can be a reliable eyewitness and provide accurate testimony.

From a practical perspective, we are at a point in the field at which we have to develop procedures that maximize the amount of accurate information, both description and identification, that is obtained from young eyewitnesses. From a theoretical perspective, what may help with the development of protocols and procedures is to understand what leads to differences in performance across age. Next, I provide some questions that are of concern to me and that may provide some fruitful seeds as we move forward in the young eyewitness field.

AGE

Perhaps one of the most important factors we must consider is age. The label *child* is a large one and can cover many years, or just a few, and it can mean different things cognitively, socially, legally, and so forth. We often make sweeping statements about *children* without defining the specific population in question. A consequence of this is not understanding the developmental progression in children's ability to describe a stranger and then to later identify that stranger. In this case, it is necessary to include children of various ages in one study using the same methodology and stimuli. The accuracy of our conclusions can be disputed when groups with large age ranges are included in studies using different methodologies and materials. In addition, differences may be exaggerated in video versus live interactions. Does the possible stress of a live event (e.g., swimming lessons; I still don't know how to swim) have a differential impact on younger and older children?

Little time is devoted to understanding the performance of eyewitnesses with developmental delays and the best procedures to use with them. Are there accommodations or considerations necessary for a 25-year-old who may be functioning as a younger person? Does developmental age affect eyewitness performance? Perhaps developmental age has a greater impact on performance than chronological age. Social support may be critical for those with developmental delays, perhaps to a greater extent than for those with a matching chronological and developmental age. Many questions must be addressed to understand better how to increase the likelihood of accurate descriptions and identifications from those with developmental delays. This is an important area of study, given the vulnerability of this population.

A neglected "child" population in the eyewitness literature is adolescence, 13 to 18 years. Legal tradition has dictated that the line between childhood and adulthood is drawn somewhere in this range; in the eyes of the law, children become adults in terms of their ability and credibility in describing and identifying perpetrators of crimes. Although in this age range children legally become adults, we do not know much about this population regarding their eyewitness abilities. The teen years are often a time to separate from family and begin to experience greater freedom from parental control. Without parents around, individuation and greater time spent with friends can lead to more chances of being involved in criminal activity, making this group vulnerable to witnessing criminal acts and/or becoming victims themselves.

Unfortunately, little attention has been paid to the adolescent eyewitness. When do adolescents become adult-like? Is the 15-year-old different from the 17-year-old or from the 19-year-old? Although the common adult group engaged to investigate eyewitness performance is often 18- to 25-year-olds (the undergraduate university student convenience sample), we know little about differences between 18- to 25-year-olds. Would we see increases in identification abilities from age 18 and onward? When does this level off? We simply do not have sufficient data with discriminations across the young adulthood to middle adulthood range. Without this, we are left to make assumptions and estimated guesses. Although this is a book about the young eyewitness, I would be remiss in not acknowledging the need for more work on post middle age eyewitness performance. This area, rich for exploration, will ultimately provide a more complete view of eyewitness testimony.

FAMILIARITY

Jacques Rivera spent more than 20 years in prison. He was identified by a 12-year-old who had seen him playing baseball several times. Johnny Williams spent 14 years in prison. He was identified by a 9-year-old victim who was his neighbor. John Stoll spent more than 25 years in prison. He was identified by several 8-year-olds who frequented his home. In all three cases, the witnesses were children, the children had some prior familiarity with the accused men, and most important, all the men were innocent (see http://www.innocenceproject.org). Despite over 100 years of research on eyewitness identification, the research has focused almost exclusively on stranger identification—that is, identifying someone never seen until the time of the crime. However, consider a caregiver at school whom a child may have seen on previous occasions but not spoken to and who is later accused of fondling the student, or a man in the park who sits on a bench watching while children play on a daily basis who a few weeks later is accused of attempting to abduct a child.

The majority of crimes against children (and adults) are committed by someone with whom the victim has some familiarity (e.g., Miethe & Drass, 1999). Recall from Chapter 1 that Elizabeth Smart's sister, Mary Katherine, witnessed her sister's abduction and noted, "I heard his voice before." It took several months for Mary Katherine to place the voice: It belonged to someone who had briefly worked for the Smarts as a gardener. In this case, the perpetrator was not known to the witness; however, neither was he a complete stranger. The degree to which Mary Katherine's previous experience with the perpetrator influenced the accuracy of her identification is unknown. Understanding how variability in an eyewitness's familiarity with the perpetrator may influence their memory accuracy (i.e., their description and identification evidence) is critical.

The main purpose of identification is to gain proof, beyond a verbal description, that the suspect is the perpetrator (Wells, 1993). Identification seems most informative in this stranger situation. However, identification is also critical for the familiar stranger. Familiarity ranges from complete stranger (i.e., never having been seen before the crime) to a very familiar other (e.g., a caregiver). Many identifications fall somewhere between these two extremes. We have almost ignored the abilities of young eyewitnesses with familiar strangers. We have to explore variations of familiarity and how familiarity affects descriptions and identifications made by the young eyewitness. This work is critically important and may be more applicable to real life than the research on strangers that has been conducted thus far.

POLICE PROCEDURES

A number of procedures have been developed and tested in an attempt to increase recall information and accurate identifications from young eyewitnesses. In attempting to increase the descriptive information given about the perpetrator, some interview protocols (those focused on open-ended recall and eliminating the use of leading questioning) can increase the likelihood of being given accurate information; however, we are still left with brief person descriptions. Researchers may have to examine ways of expanding the person descriptions provided by young eyewitness (and adults). Perhaps by using standard comparisons, (e.g., a hair color wheel), the young eyewitness may be able to provide more information. Also, more broadly, the young eyewitness may benefit from a support person or object of comfort (e.g., a favorite teddy bear) when providing descriptions and identifications. What impact would these people or objects have on the young eyewitness's abilities? It is important to consider both the cognitive and social elements for a young witness that may not be relevant or helpful to an older witness. There may be elements that can facilitate the cognitive abilities of a young witness, and social elements may be helpful in reducing uncertainty in the process, thus resulting in richer and more accurate information.

In terms of identification, no one lineup procedure seems ideal at this point, but a number of options may prove beneficial with some refinement. It should also be noted that procedures often require more than a handful of studies to explore fully their cost and benefits. At this time, I encourage further exploration into the use of the elimination procedure and the use of a wild card as an addition to a simultaneous lineup. In Chapter 4, I suggested adding a silhouette to the second judgment in the elimination procedure; this refinement may lead to improved accuracy of the young eyewitness. There may be other options as well to increase discriminability for young witnesses such that guilty perpetrators are more likely to be identified and innocent suspects are less likely to be wrongly identified.

We may also consider alternatives to binary decisions for identification. We may want to explore identification as a continuum (e.g., from 1, *not very similar*, to 10, *highly similar*) along which suspects receiving higher values have a greater likelihood of being guilty, and those receiving lower values have a decreased likelihood of guilt. We may consider changing the question we ask children from "Who committed the crime?" to "How similar is this person to the one who committed the crime?" The use of a similarity judgment or perhaps a confidence measure taken before or after the identification may also have value. However, it would be imperative to understand children's understanding of confidence. Anecdotally, after working with thousands of young participants, I am not convinced that my notion of confidence resembles a young person's response to a confidence scale, regardless of whether I use numbers, smiley faces, or rays of sunshine. If an adult notion of identification is problematic for the young eyewitness, perhaps we have to change how it is addressed or measured.

FIELD STUDIES

Most of the adult eyewitness identification research has been done using videotaped mock events. Some studies have used a live exposure in which a confederate steals an item and runs out of the room. The "classic" study involves a professor being interrupted in class by a "stranger," after which an altercation occurs or the stranger runs out with something belonging to the professor. Students in the class are the witnesses and are tested for their memory and ability to identify the stranger. A few field studies have been conducted with the use of actual eyewitnesses in live cases, with actual police officers administering the lineups. For the young eyewitness, studies have primarily consisted of either a videotape methodology or a live event, such as a swimming lesson scenario or one in which a child has to give blood and the blood is taken by a nurse who becomes the target for description and identification. Those studying the young eyewitness's abilities have been creative in selecting naturally occurring events that mimic to some degree the stress and arousal that may be present when witnessing a crime. I encourage the use of a greater variety of real-life events to understand better the young eyewitness's abilities and performance. I believe that these studies should be carried out with real young eyewitnesses. I encourage researchers to work with police and the criminal justice system to design studies that examine the abilities of young witnesses in the real world.

INDIVIDUAL DIFFERENCES

We know little about individual factors or differences that may influence an eyewitness's accuracy. Recall from the discussion of estimator versus system variables in Chapters 1 and 5 that individual differences are estimator variables. These differences are inherent to the eyewitness and cannot be changed to improve accuracy. However, a better understanding of individual differences may then suggest how a system variable can be better applied to improve accuracy. Consider how differences in introversion or shyness may interact with lineup procedure. A shy individual may be better at examining an automated lineup without anyone else in the room, whereas an individual who is not shy may do better with someone (i.e., a police officer blind to who the suspect is) there, even if the lineup is automated. Suggestibility, anxiety, depression, need for cognition (i.e., the extent to which individuals are inclined toward effortful cognitive activities), and so forth, may interact with other variables at the time of interviewing or conducting a lineup identification. Having a better understanding of individual differences in a young eyewitness may provide some direction concerning system variables to increase accuracy with description and/or identification. Individual differences that researchers may consider should be connected in some way to the processes involved in witnessing, describing, and identifying.

THE "WHY" AND THE "HOW"

Throughout this volume, you may have noticed a limited and speculative discussion of why and how differences occur. This is an area in which eyewitness researchers could expand their scope to understand better the results obtained in their studies. Studies could be designed to test theories within an eyewitness context. If we think about providing a description in simplistic terms, language develops so that we are better able to articulate what we are thinking, and we have more words to express those thoughts. We see a developmental trend for children to use more descriptors as they get older. Differences in brain development, attention, the transfer of information from short-term to long-term memory, and the ability to recall information from memory and report it accurately are all likely differences between younger and older eyewitnesses. Understanding the development of these factors is necessary but not sufficient. The development of these factors may be related to the young eyewitness's ability, but ability may not equate with performance.

The witnessing of a crime and the events that follow occur within a social context. This social context may affect the young eyewitness more so than an older eyewitness in that abilities can be suppressed to a greater extent—although a younger eyewitness may know the answers to questions and be able to provide them, other factors in the environment (e.g., wanting to please the experimenter) may cause him or her to not provide the correct answer. For example, we have to understand better the young eyewitness's propensity to guess when choosing a perpetrator from a lineup. Can this tendency for "choosing" help the young eyewitness to make a correct identification? Can we modify procedures so that the young eyewitness is less likely to choose an innocent suspect? We have to design studies to help us understand the young eyewitness's ability versus performance and the factors that influence each.

INFLUENCE IN THE COURT

The perceptions of young eyewitnesses are complex, and the prosecution of cases often rests on the testimony they provided. Although age has an influence on perceptions, there are a number of factors that interact with age, and these interactions should be explored. Real-life cases can be rich and complex; we have to explore more comprehensively these combinations of factors in small-group decision-making contexts. We have to understand better the differences in perceptions and verdicts of eyewitnesses and eyewitness–victims. We have to examine systematically two and three factors (e.g., age differences, race differences, type of crime) in combination with age along with different types of evidence, such as DNA and alibis. There are several constructs, such as reliability, honesty, credibility, trustworthiness, and accuracy, that at times are used interchangeably. However, there may be nuances to these constructs that are peculiar to the perceptions of young eyewitnesses. We have to carefully define these constructs, measure them, and understand their relation to each other. We often discuss constructs that may be related to the verdict, but ultimately, the verdict matters. We may also consider whether these constructs mediate or moderate verdicts.

CONCLUSION

We have explored some real-life cases involving young eyewitnesses and the empirical research that helps us understand the factors that may increase or decrease the completeness and accuracy of the description and identification of a stranger–perpetrator. My hope in combining real-life cases with empirical work is to illustrate that the young eyewitness can provide critical evidence to aid in the prosecution of guilty defendants. However, as with eyewitnesses of all ages, details both at the time of the event and afterward can affect the reliability of the testimony. Although we do have some knowledge of the young eyewitness, there is yet a lot to learn. I have attempted to carve out directions for future research that may lead to fruitful inquiry. I have also presented some different ideas for moving forward. It is my hope that researchers will continue to explore how we may help the young eyewitness to give more accurate evidence. I end my summary of the young eyewitness with the following thought: The young eyewitness should be valued and can provide accurate testimony when best practices are used to elicit the most reliable testimony possible.

References

Abducted child found at bottom of outhouse. (1983, August 26). *Spokane Chronicle*. Retrieved from http://news.google.com/newspapers?nid=1345&dat=19830826&id=krEvAAAAIBAJ&sjid=n_kDAAAAIBAJ&pg=5759,2375235

af Hjelmsäter, E. R., Strömwall, L. A., & Granhag, P. (2012). The self-administered interview: A means of improving children's eyewitness performance? *Psychology, Crime & Law, 18*, 897–911. http://dx.doi.org/10.1080/1068316X.2011.582844

Anastasi, J. S., & Rhodes, M. G. (2005). An own-age bias in face recognition for children and older adults. *Psychonomic Bulletin & Review, 12*, 1043–1047. http://dx.doi.org/10.3758/BF03206441

Anastasi, J. S., & Rhodes, M. G. (2006). Evidence for an own-age bias in face recognition. *North American Journal of Psychology, 8*, 237–252.

Associated Press. (1988, November 3). Man who left toddler in outhouse pit may be paroled. *AP News Archive*. Retrieved from http://www.apnewsarchive.com/1988/Man-Who-Left-Toddler-In-Outhouse-Pit-May-Be-Paroled/id-dbd0dde06328557f544cd8c63736fd68

Associated Press. (2011, May 25). Elizabeth Smart kidnapper gets life sentences. *CBC News*. Retrieved from http://www.cbc.ca/m/touch/world/story/1.1002438

Bäckman, L. (1991). Recognition memory across the adult life span: The role of prior knowledge. *Memory & Cognition, 19*, 63–71. http://dx.doi.org/10.3758/BF03198496

Barrhaven sexual assault never happened: Police. (2011, February 2). *CBC News*. Retrieved from www.cbc.ca/news/canada/ottawa/story/2011/02/02/ottawa-sexual-assault-unfounded.html

Bartlett, J. C., & Leslie, J. E. (1986). Aging and memory for faces versus single views of faces. *Memory & Cognition, 14*, 371–381. http://dx.doi.org/10.3758/BF03197012

Bassili, J. N., & Scott, B. S. (1996). Response latency as a signal to question problems in survey research. *Public Opinion Quarterly, 60*, 390–399. http://dx.doi. org/10.1086/297760

Beal, C. R., Schmitt, K. L., & Dekle, D. J. (1995). Eyewitness identification of children: Effects of absolute judgments, nonverbal response options, and event encoding. *Law and Human Behavior, 19*, 197–216. http://dx.doi.org/10.1007/ BF01499325

Behrman, B. W., & Davey, S. L. (2001). Eyewitness identification in actual criminal cases: An archival analysis. *Law and Human Behavior, 25*, 475–491. http:// dx.doi.org/10.1023/A:1012840831846

Beresford, J., & Blades, M. (2006). Children's identification of faces from lineups: The effects of lineup presentation and instructions on accuracy. *Journal of Applied Psychology, 91*, 1102–1113. http://dx.doi.org/10.1037/0021-9010.91.5.1102

Berman, G. L., Narby, D. J., & Cutler, B. L. (1995). Effects of inconsistent eyewitness statements on mock-jurors' evaluations of the eyewitness, perceptions of defendant culpability, and verdicts. *Law and Human Behavior, 19*, 79–88.

Betts, P., & Chatman, A. D. (1984, August 20). Couple thrilled at chance to save toddler. *Pittsburgh Post-Gazette.* Retrieved from http://news.google. com/newspapers?nid=1129&dat=19840820&id=69VRAAAAIBAJ&sjid= Hm4DAAAAIBAJ&pg=2849,4814588

Boon, J., & Noon, E. (1994). Changing perspectives in cognitive interviewing. *Psychology, Crime & Law, 1*, 59–69. http://dx.doi.org/10.1080/10683169408411936

Bornstein, B., & Greene, E. (2011). Jury decision making: Implications for and from psychology. *Current Directions in Psychological Science, 20*, 63–67. http:// dx.doi.org/10.1177/0963721410397282

Bottoms, B. L. (1993). Individual differences in perceptions of child sexual assault victims. In G. S. Goodman & B. L. Bottoms (Eds.), *Child victims, child witnesses: Understanding and improving testimony* (pp. 229–261). New York, NY: Guilford Press.

Bottoms, B. L., Golding, J. M., Stevenson, M. C., Wiley, T. R. A., & Yozwiak, J. A. (2007). Review of factors affections jurors' decisions in child sexual abuse cases. In M. Toglia, J. D. Read, D. F. Ross, & R. C. Lindsay (Eds.), *Handbook of eyewitness psychology: Volume I. Memory for events.* Mahwah, NJ: Erlbaum.

Bottoms, B. L., & Goodman, G. S. (1994). Perceptions of children's credibility in sexual assault cases. *Journal of Applied Social Psychology, 24*, 702–732. http:// dx.doi.org/10.1111/j.1559-1816.1994.tb00608.x

Bottoms, B., Najdowski, C., & Goodman, G. (2009). *Children as victims, witnesses, and offenders: Psychological science and the law.* New York, NY: Guilford Press.

Bottoms, B. L., Nysse-Carris, K. L., Harris, T., & Tyda, K. (2003). Jurors' perceptions of adolescent sexual assault victims who have intellectual disabilities. *Law and Human Behavior, 27,* 205–227. http://dx.doi.org/10.1023/A:1022551314668

Bower, G. H., & Karlin, M. B. (1974). Depth of processing pictures of faces and recognition memory. *Journal of Experimental Psychology, 103,* 751–757. http://dx.doi.org/10.1037/h0037190

Brainerd, C. J., Forrest, T. J., Karibian, D., & Reyna, V. F. (2006). Development of the false memory illusion. *Developmental Psychology, 42,* 962–979. http://dx.doi.org/10.1037/0012-1649.42.5.962

Brainerd, C. J., & Reyna, V. F. (1995). Learning rate, learning opportunities, and the development of forgetting. *Developmental Psychology, 31,* 251–262. http://dx.doi.org/10.1037/0012-1649.31.2.251

Brainerd, C. J., & Reyna, V. F. (1998). Fuzzy-trace theory and children's false memories. *Journal of Experimental Child Psychology, 71,* 81–129. http://dx.doi.org/10.1006/jecp.1998.2464

Brainerd, C. J., & Reyna, V. F. (2004). Fuzzy-trace theory and memory development. *Developmental Review, 24,* 396–439. http://dx.doi.org/10.1016/j.dr.2004.08.005

Brainerd, C. J., & Reyna, V. F. (Eds.). (2005). *The science of false memory.* New York, NY: Oxford University Press. http://dx.doi.org/10.1093/acprof:oso/9780195154054.001.0001

Brainerd, C. J., & Reyna, V. F. (2007). Explaining developmental reversals in false memory. *Psychological Science, 18,* 442–448. http://dx.doi.org/10.1111/j.1467-9280.2007.01919.x

Brainerd, C. J., & Reyna, V. F. (2015). Memory and knowledge. In J. G. W. Raaijmakers, A. H. Criss, R. L. Goldstone, R. M. Mosofsky, & M. Steyvers (Eds.), *Cognitive modeling in perception and memory: A Festschrift for Richard M. Shiffrin* (pp. 173–188). New York, NY: Taylor & Francis.

Brewer, N., Keast, A., & Sauer, J. D. (2010). Children's eyewitness identification performance: Effects of a *Not Sure* response option and accuracy motivation. *Legal and Criminological Psychology, 15,* 261–277. http://dx.doi.org/10.1348/135532509X474822

Brewer, N., & Wells, G. L. (2011). Eyewitness identification. *Current Directions in Psychological Science, 20,* 24–27. http://dx.doi.org/10.1177/0963721410389169

Brigham, J. C., Maass, A., Snyder, L. D., & Spaulding, K. (1982). Accuracy of eyewitness identification in a field setting. *Journal of Personality and Social Psychology, 42,* 673–681. http://dx.doi.org/10.1037/0022-3514.42.4.673

Brown, D., & Pipe, M. (2003). Variations on a technique: Enhancing children's recall using narrative elaboration training. *Applied Cognitive Psychology, 17,* 377–399. http://dx.doi.org/10.1002/acp.876

Brown, S. C., & Craik, F. I. M. (2000). Encoding and retrieval of information. In E. Tulving & F. I. M. Craik (Eds.), *The Oxford handbook of memory* (pp. 93–107). New York, NY: Oxford University Press.

Bruer, K., & Pozzulo, J. (2014). Influence of eyewitness age and recall error on mock juror decision-making. *Legal and Criminological Psychology, 19*, 332–348. http://dx.doi.org/10.1111/lcrp.12001

Candel, I., Hayne, H., Strange, D., & Prevoo, E. (2009). The effect of suggestion on children's recognition memory for seen and unseen details. *Psychology, Crime & Law, 15*, 29–39. http://dx.doi.org/10.1080/10683160802084850

Carey, S., & Diamond, R. (1977). From piecemeal to configurational representation of faces. *Science, 195*, 312–314. http://dx.doi.org/10.1126/science.831281

Carlson, C. A., & Carlson, M. A. (2012). A distinctiveness-driven reversal of the weapon-focus effect. *Applied Psychology in Criminal Justice, 8*, 36–53.

Castelli, P., Goodman, G., & Ghetti, S. (2005). Effects of interview style and witness age on perceptions of children's credibility in sexual abuse cases. *Journal of Applied Social Psychology, 35*, 297–317. http://dx.doi.org/10.1111/j.1559-1816.2005.tb02122.x

Ceci, S. J., & Bruck, M. (1993). Suggestibility of the child witness: A historical review and synthesis. *Psychological Bulletin, 113*, 403–439. http://dx.doi.org/10.1037/0033-2909.113.3.403

Ceci, S. J., & Bruck, M. (1995). *Jeopardy in the courtroom: A scientific analysis of children's testimony.* Washington, DC: American Psychological Association. http://dx.doi.org/10.1037/10180-000

Ceci, S. J., Papierno, P. B., & Kulkofsky, S. (2007). Representational constraints on children's suggestibility. *Psychological Science, 18*, 503–509. http://dx.doi.org/10.1111/j.1467-9280.2007.01930.x

Ceci, S. J., Ross, D. F., & Toglia, M. P. (1987). Suggestibility of children's memory: Psycholegal implications. *Journal of Experimental Psychology: General, 116*, 38–49. http://dx.doi.org/10.1037/0096-3445.116.1.38

Challis, B. H., Velichkovsky, B. M., & Craik, F. I. M. (1996). Levels-of-processing effects on a variety of memory tasks: New findings and theoretical implications. *Consciousness and Cognition, 5*, 142–164. http://dx.doi.org/10.1006/ccog.1996.0009

Chance, J., & Goldstein, A. (1976). Recognition of faces and verbal labels. *Bulletin of the Psychonomic Society, 7*, 384–386. http://dx.doi.org/10.3758/BF03337223

Chance, J. E., & Goldstein, A. G. (1984). Face-recognition memory: Implications for children's eyewitness testimony. *Journal of Social Issues, 40*, 69–85. http://dx.doi.org/10.1111/j.1540-4560.1984.tb01094.x

Chance, J. E., Turner, A. L., & Goldstein, A. G. (1982). Development of differential recognition for own- and other-race faces. *The Journal of Psychol-

ogy: Interdisciplinary and Applied, 112, 29–37. http://dx.doi.org/10.1080/00223980.1982.9923531

Chatman v. Mancill, 626 S.E.2d 102 (280 Ga. 253, 2006).

Clarke, A. J. B., & Butler, L. T. (2008). Dissociating word stem completion and cued recall as a function of divided attention at retrieval. *Memory, 16,* 763–772. http://dx.doi.org/10.1080/09658210802261116

Cohen, R. L., & Harnick, M. A. (1980). The susceptibility of child witnesses to suggestion: An empirical study. *Law and Human Behavior, 4,* 201–210. http://dx.doi.org/10.1007/BF01040318

Connolly, D. A., & Price, H. L. (2006). Children's suggestibility for an instance of a repeated event versus a unique event: The effect of degree of association between variable details. *Journal of Experimental Child Psychology, 93,* 207–223. http://dx.doi.org/10.1016/j.jecp.2005.06.004

Corenblum, B., & Meissner, C. A. (2006). Recognition of faces of ingroup and outgroup children and adults. *Journal of Experimental Child Psychology, 93,* 187–206. http://dx.doi.org/10.1016/j.jecp.2005.09.001

Craik, F. I. M., & Tulving, E. (1975). Depth of processing and the retention of words in episodic memory. *Journal of Experimental Psychology: General, 10,* 268–294. http://dx.doi.org/10.1037/0096-3445.104.3.268

Crookes, K., & McKone, E. (2009). Early maturity of face recognition: No childhood development of holistic processing, novel face encoding, or face-space. *Cognition, 111,* 219–247. http://dx.doi.org/10.1016/j.cognition.2009.02.004

Cross, J. F., Cross, J., & Daly, J. (1971). Sex, race, age, and beauty as factors in recognition of faces. *Perception & Psychophysics, 10,* 393–396. http://dx.doi.org/10.3758/BF03210319

Cutler, B. L., & Kovera, M. B. (2010). *Evaluating eyewitness identification.* New York, NY: Oxford University Press. http://dx.doi.org/10.1093/med:psych/9780195372687.001.0001

Cutler, B. L., Penrod, S. D., & Martens, T. K. (1987). Improving the reliability of eyewitness identifications: Putting context into context. *Journal of Applied Psychology, 72,* 629–637. http://dx.doi.org/10.1037/0021-9010.72.4.629

Dando, C., Wilcock, R., & Milne, R. (2009). The cognitive interview: The efficacy of a modified mental reinstatement of context procedure for frontline police investigators. *Applied Cognitive Psychology, 23,* 138–147. http://dx.doi.org/10.1002/acp.1451

Davies, G., & Flin, R. (1988). The accuracy and suggestibility of child witnesses. *Issues in Criminological & Legal Psychology, 13,* 21–34.

Davies, G. M., Smith, S., & Blincoe, C. (2008). A "weapon focus" effect in children. *Psychology, Crime & Law, 14,* 19–28. http://dx.doi.org/10.1080/10683160701340593

Davies, G. M., Stevenson-Robb, Y., & Flin, R. (1988). Tales out of school: Children's memory for an unexpected incident. In M. Gruneberg, P. Morris, & R. Sykes (Eds.), *Practical aspects of memory: Volume 1* (pp. 122–127). Chichester, England: Wiley.

Davies, G. M., Tarrant, A., & Flin, R. (1989). Close encounters of the witness kind: Children's memory for a simulated health inspection. *British Journal of Psychology, 80,* 415–429. http://dx.doi.org/10.1111/j.2044-8295.1989.tb02333.x

Deffenbacher, K. A., Bornstein, B. H., Penrod, S. D., & McGorty, E. K. (2004). A meta-analytic review of the effects of high stress on eyewitness memory. *Law and Human Behavior, 28,* 687–706. http://dx.doi.org/10.1007/s10979-004-0565-x

de Heering, A., de Liedekerke, C., Deboni, M., & Rossion, B. (2010). The role of experience during childhood in shaping the other-race effect. *Developmental Science, 13,* 181–187. http://dx.doi.org/10.1111/j.1467-7687.2009.00876.x

de Heering, A., Rossion, B., & Maurer, D. (2012). Developmental changes in face recognition during childhood: Evidence from upright and inverted faces. *Cognitive Development, 27,* 17–27. http://dx.doi.org/10.1016/j.cogdev.2011.07.001

Dekle, D. J., Beal, C. R., Elliott, R., & Huneycutt, D. (1996). Children as witnesses: A comparison of lineup versus showup identification methods. *Applied Cognitive Psychology, 10,* 1–12. http://dx.doi.org/10.1002/(SICI)1099-0720(199602)10:1%3C1::AID-ACP354%3E3.0.CO;2-Y

Dempsey, J. L., & Pozzulo, J. D. (2013). Children's identification accuracy of multiple perpetrators: Examining the simultaneous versus elimination line-up. *Psychiatry, Psychology, and Law, 20,* 353–365. http://dx.doi.org/10.1080/13218719.2012.679124

Dent, H. R. (1991). Experimental studies of interviewing child witnesses. In J. Doris (Ed.), *The suggestibility of children's recollections* (pp. 138–146). Washington, DC: American Psychological Association. http://dx.doi.org/10.1037/10097-008

Dent, H. R., & Stephenson, G. M. (1979). An experimental study of the effectiveness of different techniques of questioning child witnesses. *British Journal of Social & Clinical Psychology, 18,* 41–51. http://dx.doi.org/10.1111/j.2044-8260.1979.tb00302.x

Deregowski, J. B., Ellis, H. D., & Shepherd, J. W. (1975). Descriptions of White and Black faces by White and Black subjects. *International Journal of Psychology, 10,* 119–123.

Devine, D. (2012). *Jury decision making: The state of the science.* New York, NY: New York University Press.

Devine, D. J., & Caughlin, D. E. (2014). Do they matter? A meta-analytic investigation of individual characteristics and guilt judgments. *Psychology, Public Policy, and Law, 20*, 109–134. http://dx.doi.org/10.1037/law0000006

Dewhurst, S. A., & Robinson, C. A. (2004). False memories in children: Evidence for a shift from phonological to semantic associations. *Psychological Science, 15*, 782–786. http://dx.doi.org/10.1111/j.0956-7976.2004.00756.x

Diamond, R., & Carey, S. (1977). Developmental changes in the representation of faces. *Journal of Experimental Child Psychology, 23*, 1–22. http://dx.doi.org/10.1016/0022-0965(77)90069-8

Dunlevy, J. R., & Cherryman, J. (2013). Target-absent eyewitness identification line-ups: Why do children like to choose? *Psychiatry, Psychology, and Law, 20*, 284–293. http://dx.doi.org/10.1080/13218719.2012.671584

Easterbrook, J. A. (1959). The effect of emotion on cue utilization and the organization of behavior. *Psychological Review, 66*, 183–201. http://dx.doi.org/10.1037/h0047707

Elkins v. Summit County Ohio, No. 09-3680 (August 10, 2010).

Ellis, H. D. (1984). Practical aspects of face memory. In G. L. Wells & E. F. Loftus (Eds.), *Eyewitness testimony: Psychological perspectives* (pp. 12–37). New York, NY: Cambridge University Press.

Ellis, H. D. (1990). Developmental trends in face recognition. *The Psychologist, 3*, 114–119.

Ellis, H. D. (1991). *The development of face-processing skills* (Final Report to ESRC on Grant XC15250003). Retrieved from Economic and Social Research Council website: http://www.researchcatalogue.esrc.ac.uk/grants/XC15250003/outputs/read/fc8fd055-3e43-488d-a31a-4b1c63ff6fac

Ellis, H. D. (1992). The development of face-processing skills. *Philosophical Transactions of the Royal Society of London, Series B, 335*, 105–111.

Faller, K. C., Grabarek, M., Nelson-Gardell, D., & Williams, J. (2011). Techniques employed by forensic interviewers conducting extended assessments: Results from a multi-site study. *Journal of Aggression, Maltreatment & Trauma, 20*, 237–259. http://dx.doi.org/10.1080/10926771.2011.557031

Farkas, K. (2006, September 7). Man wrongly jailed files for divorce. *The Plain Dealer.* Retrieved from http://www.cleveland.com/whateverhappened/plaindealer/index.ssf?/whateverhappened/more/elkins2.html

Farrar, M. J., & Goodman, G. S. (1992). Developmental changes in event memory. *Child Development, 63*, 173–187. http://dx.doi.org/10.2307/1130911

Fawcett, J. M., Russell, E. J., Peace, K. A., & Christie, J. (2013). Of guns and geese: A meta-analytic review of the "weapon focus" literature. *Psychology, Crime & Law, 19*, 35–66. http://dx.doi.org/10.1080/1068316X.2011.599325

Feingold, A. (1994). Gender differences in personality: A meta-analysis. *Psychological Bulletin, 116,* 429–456. http://dx.doi.org/10.1037/0033-2909.116.3.429

Feinman, S., & Entwisle, D. R. (1976). Children's ability to recognize other children's faces. *Child Development, 47,* 506–510.

Finkelhor, D., Turner, H. A., Ormrod, R., Hamby, S. L., & Kracke, K. (2009). *Children's exposure to violence: A comprehensive national survey.* Washington, DC: U.S. Department of Justice, Office of Justice Programs, Office of Juvenile Justice and Delinquency Prevention.

Finkelhor, D., Turner, H., Shattuck, A., Hamby, S., & Kracke, K. (2015). *Children's exposure to violence, crime, and abuse: An update.* (OJJDP Juvenile Justice Bulletin Publication No. NCJ248547). Washington, DC: U.S. Government Printing Office.

Fisher, R. P., & Geiselman, R. E. (1992). *Memory-enhancing techniques for investigative interviewing: The cognitive interview.* Springfield, IL: Charles C Thomas.

Fitzgerald, R. J., & Price, H. L. (2015). Eyewitness identification across the life span: A meta-analysis of age differences. *Psychological Bulletin, 141,* 1228–1265. http://dx.doi.org/10.1037/bul0000013

Fitzgerald, R. J., Price, H. L., & Connolly, D. A. (2012). Anxious and nonanxious children's face identification. *Applied Cognitive Psychology, 26,* 585–593. http://dx.doi.org/10.1002/acp.2833

Fitzgerald, R. J., Whiting, B. F., Therrien, N. M., & Price, H. L. (2014). Lineup member similarity effects on children's eyewitness identification. *Applied Cognitive Psychology, 28,* 409–418. http://dx.doi.org/10.1002/acp.3012

Flexser, A. J., & Tulving, E. (1978). Retrieval independence in recognition and recall. *Psychological Review, 85,* 153–171. http://dx.doi.org/10.1037/0033-295X.85.3.153

Flin, R. H., & Shepherd, J. W. (1986). Tall stories: Eyewitnesses' ability to estimate height and weight characteristics. *Human Learning: Journal of Practical Research & Applications, 5,* 29–38.

Flowe, H. D., Mehta, A., & Ebbeson, E. B. (2011). The role of eyewitness identification evidence in felony case dispositions. *Psychology, Public Policy, and Law, 17,* 140–159. http://dx.doi.org/10.1037/a0021311

Freire, A., & Lee, K. (2001). Face recognition in 4- to 7-year-olds: Processing of configural, featural, and paraphernalia information. *Journal of Experimental Child Psychology, 80,* 347–371. http://dx.doi.org/10.1006/jecp.2001.2639

Fulton, A., & Bartlett, J. C. (1991). Young and old faces in young and old heads: The factor of age in face recognition. *Psychology and Aging, 6,* 623–630. http://dx.doi.org/10.1037/0882-7974.6.4.623

Gabbert, F., Hope, L., & Fisher, R. P. (2009). Protecting eyewitness evidence: Examining the efficacy of a self-administered interview tool. *Law and Human Behavior, 33*, 298–307. http://dx.doi.org/10.1007/s10979-008-9146-8

Garven, S., Wood, J. M., & Malpass, R. S. (2000). Allegations of wrongdoing: The effects of reinforcement on children's mundane and fantastic claims. *Journal of Applied Psychology, 85*, 38–49. http://dx.doi.org/10.1037/0021-9010.85.1.38

Geiselman, R. E. (1984). Enhancement of eyewitness memory: An empirical evaluation of the cognitive interview. *Journal of Police Science & Administration, 12*, 74–80.

Geiselman, R. E., Fisher, R. P., MacKinnon, D. P., & Holland, H. L. (1985). Eyewitness memory enhancement in the police interview: Cognitive retrieval mnemonics versus hypnosis. *Journal of Applied Psychology, 70*, 401–412. http://dx.doi.org/10.1037/0021-9010.70.2.401

Geiselman, R. E., & Padilla, J. (1988). Cognitive interviewing with child witnesses. *Journal of Police Science & Administration, 16*, 236–242.

Gilligan, C. (1982). *In a different voice: Psychological theory and women's development.* Cambridge, MA: Harvard University Press.

Golding, J. M., Bradshaw, G. S., Dunlap, E. E., & Hodell, E. C. (2007). The impact of mock jury gender composition on deliberations and conviction rates in a child sexual assault trial. *Child Maltreatment, 12*, 182–190. http://dx.doi.org/10.1177/1077559506298995

Goldstein, A. G., Johnson, K. S., & Chance, J. E. (1979). Does fluency of face description imply superior face recognition? *Bulletin of the Psychonomic Society, 13*, 15–18. http://dx.doi.org/10.3758/BF03334999

Goleman, D. (1984, November 6). Studies of children as witnesses find surprising accuracy. *The New York Times.* Retrieved from http://www.nytimes.com/1984/11/06/science/studies-of-children-as-witnesses-find-surprising-accuracy.html

Gonzalez, R., Ellsworth, P. C., & Pembroke, M. (1993). Response biases in lineups and showups. *Journal of Personality and Social Psychology, 64*, 525–537. http://dx.doi.org/10.1037/0022-3514.64.4.525

Goodman, G. S., Bottoms, B. L., Herscovici, B., & Shaver, P. (1989). Determinants of the child victim's perceived credibility. In S. J Ceci, D. F. Ross, & M. P. Toglia (Eds.), *Perspectives on children's testimony* (pp. 1–22). New York, NY: Springer-Verlag.

Goodman, G. S., Golding, J. M., & Haith, M. M. (1984). Jurors' reactions to child witnesses. *Journal of Social Issues, 40*, 139–156.

Goodman, G. S., Golding, J. M., Helgeson, V. S., Haith, M. M., & Michelli, J. (1987). When a child takes the witness stand: Jurors' perceptions of children's eyewitness testimony. *Law and Human Behavior, 11*, 27–40.

Goodman, G. S., Quas, J. A., Batterman-Faunce, J., Riddlesberger, M. M., & Kuhn, J. (1994). Predictors of accurate and inaccurate memories of traumatic events experienced in childhood. *Consciousness and Cognition, 3,* 269–294. http://dx.doi.org/10.1006/ccog.1994.1016

Goodman, G. S., Sayfan, L., Lee, J. S., Sandhei, M., Walle-Olsen, A., Magnussen, S., & Arredondo, P. (2007). The development of memory for own- and other-race faces. *Journal of Experimental Child Psychology, 98,* 233–242. http://dx.doi.org/10.1016/j.jecp.2007.08.004

Greene, E. (1988). Judge's instructions on eyewitness testimony: Evaluation and revision. *Journal of Applied Social Psychology, 18,* 252–276.

Gronlund, S. D., Carlson, C. A., Dailey, S. B., & Goodsell, C. A. (2009). Robustness of the sequential lineup advantage. *Journal of Experimental Psychology: Applied, 15,* 140–152. http://dx.doi.org/10.1037/a0015082

Gronlund, S. D., Carlson, C. A., Neuschatz, J. S., Goodsell, C. A., Wetmore, S. A., Wooten, A., Graham, M. (2012). Showups versus lineups: An evaluation using ROC Analysis. *Journal of Applied Research in Memory and Cognition, 1,* 221–228. http://dx.doi.org/10.1016/j.jarmac.2012.09.003

Gronlund, S. D., Wixted, J. T., & Mickes, L. (2014). Evaluating eyewitness identification procedures using receiver operating characteristic analysis. *Current Directions in Psychological Science, 23,* 3–10. http://dx.doi.org/10.1177/0963721413498891

Hardy, C. L., & Van Leeuwen, S. A. (2004). Interviewing young children: Effects of probe structures and focus of rapport-building talk on the qualities of young children's eyewitness statements. *Canadian Journal of Behavioural Science/Revue Canadienne Des Sciences Du Comportement, 36,* 155–165. http://dx.doi.org.proxy.library.carleton.ca/10.1037/h0087226

Havard, C., & Memon, A. (2013). The mystery man can help reduce false identifications for child witnesses: Evidence from video line-ups. *Applied Cognitive Psychology, 27,* 50–59. http://dx.doi.org/10.1002/acp.2870

He, Y., Ebner, N., & Johnson, M. K. (2011). What predicts the own-age bias in face recognition memory? *Social Cognition, 29,* 97–109. http://dx.doi.org/10.1521/soco.2011.29.1.97

Holcomb, M. J., & Jacquin, K. M. (2007). Juror perceptions of child eyewitness testimony in a child sexual abuse trial. *Journal of Child Sexual Abuse, 16,* 79–95. http://dx.doi.org/10.1300/J070v16n02_05

Holliday, R. E., & Albon, A. J. (2004). Minimising misinformation effects in young children with cognitive interview mnemonics. *Applied Cognitive Psychology, 18,* 263–281. http://dx.doi.org/10.1002/acp.973

Home Office and The Rt Hon Nick Herbert. (2011, February 21). Police and Criminal Evidence Act Code D 2011. Retrieved from https://www.gov.uk/government/publications/pace-code-d-2011

Humphries, J. E., Holliday, R. E., & Flowe, H. D. (2012). Faces in motion: Age-related changes in eyewitness identification performance in simultaneous, sequential, and elimination video lineups. *Applied Cognitive Psychology*, *26*, 149–158. http://dx.doi.org/10.1002/acp.1808

Innocence Project. (n.d.). *Clarence Elkins*. Retrieved from http://www.innocenceproject.org/cases/clarence-elkins

Jack, F., Leov, J., & Zajac, R. (2014). Age-related differences in the free-recall accounts of child, adolescent, and adult witnesses. *Applied Cognitive Psychology*, *28*, 30–38. http://dx.doi.org/10.1002/acp.2951

James, S. (2007, February 11). Killer Instinct. *NBC News*. Retrieved from http://www.nbcnews.com/id/17562131/ns/dateline_nbc-killer_instinct/t/killer-instinct/#.Vrj7UTZllYh

Karageorge, A., & Zajac, R. (2011). Exploring the effects of age and delay on children's person identifications: Verbal descriptions, lineup performance, and the influence of wildcards. *British Journal of Psychology*, *102*, 161–183. http://dx.doi.org/10.1348/000712610X507902

Kask, K., & Bull, R. (2009). The effects of different presentation methods on multi-ethnicity face recognition. *Psychology, Crime & Law*, *15*, 73–89. http://dx.doi.org/10.1080/10683160802131131

Kask, K., Bull, R., Heinla, I., & Davies, G. (2007). The effect of a standard to improve person descriptions by children. *Journal of Police and Criminal Psychology*, *22*, 77–83. http://dx.doi.org/10.1007/s11896-007-9008-1

Katz, C., & Hershkowitz, I. (2012). The effect of multipart prompts on children's testimonies in sexual abuse investigations. *Child Abuse & Neglect*, *36*, 753–759. http://dx.doi.org/10.1016/j.chiabu.2012.07.002

Kidnapped child, 3, able to pick out her abductor. (1983, September 7). *The Bulletin*. Retrieved from http://news.google.com/newspapers?nid=1243&dat=19830907&id=eqNYAAAAIBAJ&ssji=qoYDAAAAIBAJ&pg=5015,5286264

King, M. A., & Yuille, J. C. (1987). Suggestibility and the child witness. In S. J. Ceci, M. P. Toglia, & D. F. Ross (Eds.), *Children's eyewitness memory* (pp. 24–35). New York, NY: Springer-Verlag. http://dx.doi.org/10.1007/978-1-4684-6338-5_2

Kirby v. Illinois, 406 U.S. 682 (1972).

Köhnken, G., Milne, R., Memon, A., & Bull, R. (1999). The cognitive interview: A meta-analysis. *Psychology, Crime & Law*, *5*, 3–27. http://dx.doi.org/10.1080/10683169908414991

Lamb, M. E., Hershkowitz, I., Orbach, Y., & Esplin, P. W. (2008). *Tell me what happened: Structured investigative interviews of child victims and witnesses.* West Sussex, England: Wiley. http://dx.doi.org/10.1002/9780470773291

Lampinen, J. M., Copeland, S. M., & Neuschatz, J. S. (2011). Recollections of things schematic: Room schemas revisited. *Journal of Experimental Psychology: Learning, Memory, and Cognition, 27,* 1211–1222. http://dx.doi.org/10.1037/0278-7393.27.5.1211

Leippe, M. R., & Romanczyk, A. (1989). Reactions to child (versus adult) eyewitnesses: The influence of jurors' preconceptions and witness behavior. *Law and Human Behavior, 13,* 103–132. http://dx.doi.org/10.1007/BF01055919

Leung, R. (2009, February 11). Star witness: Is Clarence Elkins guilty of murder? *Forty Eight Hours.* Retrieved from www.cbsnews.com/8301-18559_162-570032.html

Lindberg, M. A., Chapman, M. T., Samsock, D., Thomas, S. W., & Lindberg, A. W. (2003). Comparisons of three different investigative interview techniques with young children. *The Journal of Genetic Psychology: Research and Theory on Human Development, 164,* 5–28. http://dx.doi.org.proxy.library.carleton.ca/10.1080/00221320309597500

Lindberg, M. A., Jones, S., McComas Collard, L., & Thomas, S. W. (2001). Similarities and differences in eyewitness testimonies of children who directly versus vicariously experience stress. *The Journal of Genetic Psychology: Research and Theory on Human Development, 162,* 314–333. http://dx.doi.org/10.1080/00221320109597486

Lindsay, R. C. L., Mansour, J. K., Beaudry, J. L., Leach, A., & Bertrand, M. I. (2009). Sequential lineup presentation: Patterns and policy. *Legal and Criminological Psychology, 14,* 13–24. http://dx.doi.org/10.1348/135532508X382708

Lindsay, R. C. L., Martin, R., & Webber, L. (1994). Default values in eyewitness descriptions: A problem for the match-to-description lineup foil selection strategy. *Law and Human Behavior, 18,* 527–541. http://dx.doi.org/10.1007/BF01499172

Lindsay, R. C. L., Pozzulo, J. D., Craig, W., Lee, K., & Corber, S. (1997). Simultaneous lineups, sequential lineups, and showups: Eyewitness identification decisions of adults and children. *Law and Human Behavior, 21,* 391–404. http://dx.doi.org/10.1023/A:1024807202926

Lindsay, R. C., & Wells, G. L. (1985). Improving eyewitness identifications from lineups: Simultaneous versus sequential lineup presentation. *Journal of Applied Psychology, 70,* 556–564. http://dx.doi.org/10.1037/0021-9010.70.3.556

List, J. (1986). Age and schematic differences in the reliability of eyewitness testimony. *Developmental Psychology, 22,* 50–57. http://dx.doi.org/10.1037/0012-1649.22.1.50

Lowenstein, J. A., Blank, H., & Sauer, J. D. (2010). Uniforms affect the accuracy of children's eyewitness identification decisions. *Journal of Investigative Psychology and Offender Profiling, 7,* 59–73. http://dx.doi.org/10.1002/jip.104

Luus, C. A. E., & Wells, G. L. (1991). Eyewitness identification and the selection of distracters for lineups. *Law and Human Behavior, 15,* 43–57. http://dx.doi.org/10.1007/BF01044829

Malpass, R. S., & Devine, P. G. (1981). Eyewitness identification: Lineup instructions and the absence of the offender. *Journal of Applied Psychology, 66,* 482–489. http://dx.doi.org/10.1037/0021-9010.66.4.482

Malpass, R. S., & Kravitz, J. (1969). Recognition for faces of own and other race. *Journal of Personality and Social Psychology, 13,* 330–334. http://dx.doi.org/10.1037/h0028434

Malpass, R. S., Lavigueur, H., & Weldon, D. (1973). Verbal and visual training in face recognition. *Perception & Psychophysics, 14,* 285–292. http://dx.doi.org/10.3758/BF03212392

Malpass, R. S., Ross, S. J., Meissner, C. A., & Marcon, J. L. (2009). The need for expert psychological testimony on eyewitness identification. In B. L. Cutler (Ed.), *Expert testimony on the psychology of eyewitness identification* (pp. 3–27). New York, NY: Oxford University Press. http://dx.doi.org/10.1093/acprof:oso/9780195331974.003.001

Mancill v. State, 554 S.E.2d 477 (274 GA 465) (2001).

Marin, B. V., Holmes, D. L., Guth, M., & Kovac, P. (1979). The potential of children as eyewitnesses: A comparison of children and adults on eyewitness tasks. *Law and Human Behavior, 3,* 295–306. http://dx.doi.org/10.1007/BF01039808

Marschark, M., & Hunt, R. R. (1989). A re-examination of the role of imagery in learning and memory. *Journal of Experimental Psychology: Learning, Memory, and Cognition, 15,* 710–720.

Mastroberardino, S., Natali, V., & Candel, I. (2012). The effect of eye closure on children's eyewitness testimonies. *Psychology, Crime & Law, 18,* 245–257. http://dx.doi.org/10.1080/10683161003801100

McCauley, M. R., & Parker, J. F. (2001). When will a child be believed? The impact of the victim's age and juror's gender on children's credibility and verdict in a sexual-abuse case. *Child Abuse and Neglect, 25,* 523–529.

McFarland, S., & Falk, A. (2010, November 10). The testimony of Elizabeth Smart. *The Salt Lake Tribune.* Retrieved from http://www.sltrib.com/sltrib/home3/50639245-76/elizabeth-mitchell-smart-viti.html.csp

McQuiston-Surrett, D., Malpass, R. S., & Tredoux, C. G. (2006). Sequential vs. simultaneous lineups: A review of methods, data, and theory. *Psychology, Public Policy, and Law, 12,* 137–169. http://dx.doi.org/10.1037/1076-8971.12.2.137

Mecklenburg, S. H., Bailey, P. J., & Larson, M. R. (2008). The Illinois field study: A significant contribution to understanding real world eyewitness identification Issues. *Law and Human Behavior, 32,* 22–27. http://dx.doi.org/10.1007/s10979-007-9108-6

Meissner, C. A., & Brigham, J. C. (2001). Thirty years of investigating the own-race bias in memory for faces: A meta-analytic review. *Psychology, Public Policy, and Law, 7,* 3–35. http://dx.doi.org/10.1037/1076-8971.7.1.3

Melnyk, L., Crossman, A. M., & Scullin, M. H. (2007). The suggestibility of children's memory. *The handbook of eyewitness psychology: Vol. I. Memory for events* (pp. 401–427). Mahwah, NJ: Erlbaum.

Memon, A., & Bull, R. (1991). The cognitive interview: Its origins, empirical support, evaluation and practical implications. *Journal of Community & Applied Social Psychology, 1,* 291–307. http://dx.doi.org/10.1002/casp.2450010405

Memon, A., Cronin, O., Eaves, R., & Bull, R. (1993). The cognitive interview and child witnesses. *Issues in Criminological & Legal Psychology, 20,* 3–9.

Memon, A., Meissner, C. A., & Fraser, J. (2010). The cognitive interview: A meta-analytic review and study space analysis of the past 25 years. *Psychology, Public Policy, and Law, 16,* 340–372. http://dx.doi.org/10.1037/a0020518

Memon, A., & Rose, R. (2002). Identification abilities of children: Does a verbal description hurt face recognition? *Psychology, Crime & Law, 8,* 229–242. http://dx.doi.org/10.1080/10683160208401817

Mickes, L., Flowe, H. D., & Wixted, J. T. (2012). Receiver operating characteristic analysis of eyewitness memory: Comparing the diagnostic accuracy of simultaneous versus sequential lineups. *Journal of Experimental Psychology: Applied, 18,* 361–376. http://dx.doi.org/10.1037/a0030609

Miethe, T. D., & Drass, K. A. (1999). Exploring the social context of instrumental and expressive homicides: An application of qualitative comparative analysis. *Journal of Quantitative Criminology, 1,* 1–21. http://dx.doi.org/10.1023/A:1007550704282

Mitchell, K. J., Livosky, M., & Mather, M. (1998). The weapon focus effect revisited: The role of novelty. *Legal and Criminological Psychology, 3,* 287–303. http://dx.doi.org/10.1111/j.2044-8333.1998.tb00367.x

Mondani, M. S., Pellegrino, J. W., & Battig, W. F. (1973). Free and cued recall as a function of different levels of word processing. *Journal of Experimental Psychology, 101,* 324–329. http://dx.doi.org/10.1037/h0035250

Morgan, E. (2011, August 31). Elizabeth Smart kidnapper Brian David Mitchell leaves Utah for federal prison. *KLS News.* Retrieved from http://www.ksl.com/?sid=17053523

Moses, J. (2010, November 8). The abduction of Elizabeth Smart: Her own story. *TIME.* Retrieved from http://content.time.com/time/nation/article/0,8599,2030204,00.html

Neil v. Biggers, 409 U.S. 188 (1972).

Nelson, K. E., & Kosslyn, S. M. (1976). Recognition of previously labeled or unlabeled pictures by 5-year-olds and adults. *Journal of Experimental Child Psychology, 21,* 40–45. http://dx.doi.org/10.1016/0022-0965(76)90055-2

Ng, W., & Lindsay, R. C. L. (1994). Cross-race facial recognition: Failure of the contact hypothesis. *Journal of Cross-Cultural Psychology, 25,* 217–232. http://dx.doi.org/10.1177/0022022194252004

Nicholson, A. S., Yarbrough, A. M., & Penrod, S. D. (2014). Jury decision making and eyewitness testimony. In G. Bruinsma & D. Weisburd (Eds.), *Encyclopedia of criminology and criminal justice* (pp. 2727–2735). New York, NY: Springer.

Nightingale, N. (1993). Reactions to child victim witnesses: Factors affecting trial outcome. *Law and Human Behavior, 17,* 679–694. http://dx.doi.org/10.1007/BF01044689

Nigro, G. N., Buckley, M. A., Hill, D. A., & Nelson, J. (1989). When juries "hear" children testify: The effects of eyewitness age and speech style on jurors' perceptions of testimony. In S. J. Ceci, D. F. Ross, & M. P. Toglia (Eds.), *Perspectives on children's testimony* (pp. 57–70). New York, NY: Springer-Verlag.

Nuñez, N., Kehn, A., & Wright, D. (2011). When children are witnesses: The effects of context, age, and gender on perceptions of cognitive ability and honesty. *Applied Cognitive Psychology, 25,* 460–468. http://dx.doi.org/10.1002/acp.1713

O'Neill, A. (2013, August 12). *The coldest case ever solved.* Retrieved from http://myfox8.com/2013/08/12/the-coldest-case-ever-solved/

O'Neill, M. C., & Pozzulo, J. D. (2012). Jurors' judgments across multiple identifications and descriptor inconsistencies. *American Journal of Forensic Psychology, 30,* 39–66.

Orbach, Y., Hershkowitz, I., Lamb, M. E., Sternberg, K. J., Esplin, P. W., & Horowitz, D. (2000). Assessing the value of structured protocols for forensic interviews of alleged child abuse victims. *Child Abuse & Neglect, 24,* 733–752. http://dx.doi.org/10.1016/S0145-2134(00)00137-X

Parker, A., Dagnall, N., & Munley, G. (2012). Encoding tasks dissociate the effects of divided attention on category-cued recall and category-exemplar generation. *Experimental Psychology, 59,* 124–131. http://dx.doi.org/10.1027/1618-3169/a000134.

Parker, J. F., & Carranza, L. E. (1989). Eyewitness testimony of children in target-present and target-absent lineups. *Law and Human Behavior, 13,* 133–149. http://dx.doi.org/10.1007/BF01055920

Parker, J. F., Haverfield, E., & Baker-Thomas, S. (1986). Eyewitness testimony of children. *Journal of Applied Social Psychology, 16,* 287–302.

Parker, J. F., & Myers, A. (2001). Attempts to improve children's identification from sequential-presentation lineups. *Journal of Applied Social Psychology, 31,* 796–815. http://dx.doi.org/10.1111/j.1559-1816.2001.tb01414.x

Parker, J. F., & Ryan, V. (1993). An attempt to reduce guessing behavior in children's and adults' eyewitness identifications. *Law and Human Behavior, 17,* 11–26. http://dx.doi.org/10.1007/BF01044534

Peled, M., Iarocci, G., & Connolly, D. A. (2004). Eyewitness testimony and perceived credibility of youth with mild intellectual disability. *Journal of Intellectual Disability Research, 48,* 699–703. http://dx.doi.org/10.1111/j.1365-2788.2003.00559.x

People v. McCullough, No. 11 CF 454 (2012).

People v. Thiret, 685 P.2d 193, No. 84SA107 (1984).

Peterson, C., & Bell, M. (1996). Children's memory for traumatic injury. *Child Development, 67,* 3045–3070. http://dx.doi.org/10.2307/1131766

Peterson, C., & Biggs, M. (1997). Interviewing children about trauma: Problems with "specific" questions. *Journal of Traumatic Stress, 10,* 279–290. http://dx.doi.org/10.1002/jts.2490100208

Pezdek, K., Blandon-Gitlin, I., & Moore, C. (2003). Children's face recognition memory: More evidence for the cross-race effect. *Journal of Applied Psychology, 88,* 760–763. http://dx.doi.org/10.1037/0021-9010.88.4.760

Pezdek, K., & Stolzenberg, S. (2014). Are individuals' familiarity judgments diagnostic of prior contact? *Psychology, Crime & Law, 20,* 302–314. http://dx.doi.org/10.1080/1068316X.2013.772181

Pickel, K. L. (1998). Unusualness and threat as possible causes of "weapon focus." *Memory, 6,* 277–295. http://dx.doi.org/10.1080/741942361

Pickel, K. L. (1999). The influence of context on the "weapon focus" effect. *Law and Human Behavior, 23,* 299–311. http://dx.doi.org/10.1023/A:1022356431375

Pickel, K. L., Narter, D. B., Jameson, M. M., & Lenhardt, T. T. (2008). The weapon focus effect in child eyewitnesses. *Psychology, Crime & Law, 14,* 61–72. http://dx.doi.org/10.1080/10683160701391307

Pickel, K. L., Ross, S. J., & Truelove, R. S. (2006). Do weapons automatically capture attention? *Applied Cognitive Psychology, 20,* 871–893. http://dx.doi.org/10.1002/acp.1235

Pigott, M. A., & Brigham, J. C. (1985). Relationship between accuracy of prior description and facial recognition. *Journal of Applied Psychology, 70,* 547–555. http://dx.doi.org/10.1037/0021-9010.70.3.547

Pigott, M. A., Brigham, J. C., & Bothwell, R. K. (1990). A field study on the relationship between quality of eyewitnesses' descriptions and identification accuracy. *Journal of Police Science and Administration, 17,* 84–88.

Platz, S. J., & Hosch, H. M. (1988). Cross-racial/ethnic eyewitness identification: A field study. *Journal of Applied Social Psychology, 18,* 972–984. http://dx.doi.org/10.1111/j.1559-1816.1988.tb01187.x

Poole, D. A., & Lindsay, D. S. (1995). Interviewing preschoolers: Effects of non-suggestive techniques, parental coaching, and leading questions on reports of nonexperienced events. *Journal of Experimental Child Psychology, 60,* 129–154.

Possley, M. (n.d.). Clarence Elkins. *National Registry of Exonerations.* Retrieved from http://www.law.umich.edu/special/exoneration/Pages/casedetail.aspx?caseid=3202

Pozzulo, J. D., & Balfour, J. (2006). The impact of change in appearance on children's eyewitness identification accuracy: Comparing simultaneous and elimination lineup procedures. *Legal and Criminological Psychology, 11,* 25–34.

Pozzulo, J. D., & Dempsey, J. (2006). Biased lineup instructions: Examining the effect of pressure on children's and adults' eyewitness identification accuracy. *Journal of Applied Social Psychology, 36,* 1381–1394. http://dx.doi.org/10.1111/j.0021-9029.2006.00064.x

Pozzulo, J. D., & Dempsey, J. (2009a). Could target age explain identification accuracy differences between child and adult eyewitnesses? *Psychiatry, Psychology and Law, 16,* S137–S144. http://dx.doi.org.proxy.library.carleton.ca/10.1080/13218710802620414

Pozzulo, J. D., & Dempsey, J. (2009b). Witness factors and their influence on jurors' perceptions and verdicts. *Criminal Justice and Behavior, 36,* 923–934. http://dx.doi.org/10.1177/0093854809338450

Pozzulo, J. D., Dempsey, J., Bruer, K., & Sheahan, C. (2012). The culprit in target-absent lineups: Understanding young children's false positive responding. *Journal of Police and Criminal Psychology, 27,* 55–62. http://dx.doi.org/10.1007/s11896-011-9089-8

Pozzulo, J. D., Dempsey, J., & Crescini, C. (2009). Preschoolers' person description and identification accuracy: A comparison of the simultaneous and elimination lineup procedures. *Journal of Applied Developmental Psychology, 30,* 667–676. http://dx.doi.org/10.1016/j.appdev.2009.01.004

Pozzulo, J. D., Dempsey, J. L., Crescini, C., & Lemieux, J. M. T. (2009). Examining the relation between eyewitness recall and recognition for children and adults. *Psychology, Crime & Law, 15,* 409–424. http://dx.doi.org/10.1080/10683160802279625

Pozzulo, J. D., Dempsey, J. L., O'Neill, M., & Grech, D. (2009). The relationship between recalling a person and recognizing that person. *American Journal of Forensic Psychology, 27,* 19–36.

Pozzulo, J. D., Dempsey, J., & Pettalia, J. (2013). The Z generation: Examining perpetrator descriptions and lineup identification procedures. *Journal of Police and Criminal Psychology, 28,* 63–74. http://dx.doi.org/10.1007/s11896-012-9107-5

Pozzulo, J. D., Dempsey, J. L., & Wells, K. (2010). Does lineup size matter with child witnesses. *Journal of Police and Criminal Psychology, 25,* 22–26. http://dx.doi.org/10.1007/s11896-009-9055-x

Pozzulo, J. D., & Lindsay, R. C. L. (1997). Increasing correct identifications by children. *Expert Evidence, 5,* 126–132. http://dx.doi.org/10.1023/A:1008875802767

Pozzulo, J. D., & Lindsay, R. C. L. (1998). Identification accuracy of children versus adults: A meta-analysis. *Law and Human Behavior, 22,* 549–570. http://dx.doi.org/10.1023/A:1025739514042

Pozzulo, J. D., & Lindsay, R. C. L. (1999). Elimination lineups: An improved identification procedure for child eyewitnesses. *Journal of Applied Psychology, 84,* 167–176. http://dx.doi.org/10.1037/0021-9010.84.2.167

Pozzulo, J. D., Pettalia, J. L., Bruer, K., & Javaid, S. (2014). Eyewitness age and familiarity with the defendant: Influential factors in mock jurors' assessments of defendant guilt? *American Journal of Forensic Psychology, 32,* 39–51.

Pozzulo, J. D., & Warren, K. L. (2003). Descriptions and identifications of strangers by youth and adult eyewitnesses. *Journal of Applied Psychology, 88,* 315–323. http://dx.doi.org/10.1037/0021-9010.88.2.315

Quas, J. A., Bottoms, B. L., Haegerich, T., & Nysse-Carris, K. (2002). Effects of child and defendant gender on juror decision making in child sexual abuse trials. *Journal of Applied Social Psychology, 32,* 1993–2021.

Quas, J. A., Rush, E. B., Yim, I. S., & Nikolayev, M. (2014). Effects of stress on memory in children and adolescents: Testing causal connections. *Memory, 22,* 616–632. http://dx.doi.org/10.1080/09658211.2013.809766

Quas, J. A., Schaaf, J. M., Alexander, K. W., & Goodman, G. S. (2000). Do you really remember it happening or do you only remember being asked about it happening? Children's source monitoring in forensic contexts. In K. P. Roberts & M. Blades (Eds.), *Children's source monitoring* (pp. 197–226). Mahwah, NJ: Erlbaum.

R v. Sinclair, SCC 35 (2010).

Ramsland, K. (n.d.). *Shadow of a doubt: The Clarence Elkins story.* Retrieved from http://www.trutv.com/library/crime/criminal_mind/forensics/ff313_clarence_elkins/1_index.html

Reiselman, D. (2006, February). Wrongfully imprisoned man thanks UC students for freedom. *UC Magazine.* Retrieved from http://magazine.uc.edu/editors_picks/recent_features/Innocence/elkins.html

Reiselman, D. (2013, October). Ohio innocence project at UC advocates for the innocent. *UC Magazine.* Retrieved from http://magazine.uc.edu/editors_picks/recent_features/Innocence/OIP.html

Reyna, V. F., & Kiernan, B. (1994). Development of gist versus verbatim memory in sentence recognition: Effects of lexical familiarity, semantic content, encoding instructions, and retention interval. *Developmental Psychology, 30*, 178–191. http://dx.doi.org/10.1037/0012-1649.30.2.178

Rhodes, M. G., & Anastasi, J. S. (2012). The own-age bias in face recognition: A meta-analytic and theoretical review. *Psychological Bulletin, 138*, 146–174. http://dx.doi.org/10.1037/a0025750

Roebers, C. M., Bjorklund, D. F., Schneider, W., & Cassel, W. S. (2002). Differences and similarities in event recall and suggestibility between children and adults in Germany and the United States. *Experimental Psychology, 49*, 132–140. http://dx.doi.org/10.1027//1618-3169.49.2.132

Roebers, C. M., & Schneider, W. (2001). Memory for an observed event in the presence of prior misinformation: Developmental patterns of free recall and identification accuracy. *British Journal of Developmental Psychology, 19*, 507–524. http://dx.doi.org/10.1348/026151001166227

Ross, D. F., Dunning, D., Toglia, M., & Ceci, S. (1990). The child in the eyes of the jury: Assessing mock jurors' perceptions of the child witness. *Law and Human Behavior, 14*, 5–23. http://dx.doi.org/10.1007/BF01055786

Ross, D. F., Jurden, F. H., Lindsay, R. C. L., & Keeney, J. M. (2003). Replications and limitations of a two-factor model of child witness credibility. *Journal of Applied Social Psychology, 32*, 418–431. http://dx.doi.org/10.1111/j.1559-1816.2003.tb01903.x

Rowland, R. B. (2005, September). History of the Sheridan police department in Sheridan Colorado. *Rootsweb*. Retrieved from http://www.rootsweb.ancestry.com/~coshs/ha_police.htm

Rush, E. B., Quas, J. A., Yim, I. S., Nikolayev, M., Clark, S. E., & Larson, R. P. (2014). Stress, interviewer support, and children's eyewitness identification accuracy. *Child Development, 85*, 1292–1305. http://dx.doi.org/10.1111/cdev.12177

Ruva, C. L., & Bryant, J. B. (2004). The impact of age, speech style, and question form on perceptions of witness credibility and trial outcome. *Journal of Applied Social Psychology, 34*, 1919–1944. http://dx.doi.org/10.1111/j.1559-1816.2004.tb02593.x

Saywitz, K. J., & Snyder, L. (1996). Narrative elaboration: Test of a new procedure for interviewing children. *Journal of Consulting and Clinical Psychology, 64*, 1347–1357. http://dx.doi.org/10.1037/0022-006X.64.6.1347

Schmidt, C. W., & Brigham, J. C. (1996). Jurors' perceptions of child victim–witnesses in a simulated sexual abuse trial. *Law and Human Behavior, 20*, 581–606.

Schutte, J. W., & Hosch, H. M. (1997). Gender differences in sexual assault verdicts: A meta-analysis. *Journal of Social Behavior and Personality, 12,* 759–722.

Semmler, C., & Brewer, N. (2002). Effects of mood and emotion on juror processing and judgments. *Behavioral Sciences & the Law, 20,* 423–436. http://dx.doi.org/10.1002/bsl.502

Shepherd, J. W., & Deregowski, J. B. (1981). Races and faces—A comparison of the responses of Africans and Europeans to faces of the same and different races. *British Journal of Social Psychology, 20,* 125–133. http://dx.doi.org/10.1111/j.2044-8309.1981.tb00485.x

Sister recounts how she helped find Elizabeth Smart. (2005, July 21). *ABC News.* Retrieved from http://abcnews.go.com/Primetime/story?id=965906&page=1

Slone, A. E., Brigham, J. C., & Meissner, C. A. (2000). Social and cognitive factors affecting the own-race bias in Whites. *Basic and Applied Social Psychology, 22,* 71–84. http://dx.doi.org/10.1207/S15324834BASP2202_1

Spanos, N., Myers, B., DuBreuil, S., & Pawlak, A. (1992). The effects of polygraph evidence and eyewitness testimony on the beliefs and decisions of mock jurors. *Imagination, Cognition and Personality, 12,* 103–113. http://dx.doi.org/10.2190/1AB2-3WLX-BFY1-8YCP

Sparling, J., Wilder, D. A., Kondash, J., Boyle, M., & Compton, M. (2011). Effects of interviewer behavior on accuracy of children's responses. *Journal of Applied Behavior Analysis, 44,* 587–592. http://dx.doi.org/10.1901/jaba.2011.44-587

Sporer, S. L. (1996). Psychological aspects of person descriptions. In S. L. Sporer, R. S., Malpass, & G. Koehnken (Eds.), *Psychological issues in eyewitness identification* (pp. 53–86). Hillsdale, NJ: Erlbaum.

Sporer, S. L. (2001a). The cross-race effect: Beyond recognition of faces in the laboratory. *Psychology, Public Policy, and Law, 7,* 170–200. http://dx.doi.org/10.1037/1076-8971.7.1.170

Sporer, S. L. (2001b). Recognizing faces of other ethnic groups: An integration of theories. *Psychology, Public Policy, and Law, 7,* 36–97. http://dx.doi.org/10.1037/1076-8971.7.1.36

Sporer, S. L., Penrod, S., Read, D., & Cutler, B. (1995). Choosing, confidence, and accuracy: A meta-analysis of the confidence–accuracy relation in eyewitness identification studies. *Psychological Bulletin, 118,* 315–327. http://dx.doi.org/10.1037/0033-2909.118.3.315

Sporer, S. L., Trinkl, B., & Guberova, E. (2007). Matching faces: Differences in processing speed of out-group faces by different ethnic groups. *Journal of Cross-Cultural Psychology, 38,* 398–412. http://dx.doi.org/10.1177/0022022107302310

State v. Guard, No. 20100720-CA (2013).

Steblay, N. M. (1992). A meta-analytic review of the weapon focus effect. *Law and Human Behavior, 16*, 413–424. http://dx.doi.org/10.1007/BF02352267

Steblay, N. M. (1997). Social influence in eyewitness recall: A meta-analytic review of lineup instruction effects. *Law and Human Behavior, 21*, 283–297. http://dx.doi.org/10.1023/A:1024890732059

Steblay, N., Dysart, J., Fulero, S., & Lindsay, R. C. L. (2001). Eyewitness accuracy rates in sequential and simultaneous lineup presentations: A meta-analytic comparison. *Law and Human Behavior, 25*, 459–473. http://dx.doi.org/10.1023/A:1012888715007

Steblay, N., Dysart, J., Fulero, S., & Lindsay, R. C. L. (2003). Eyewitness accuracy rates in police showup and lineup presentations: A meta-analytic comparison. *Law and Human Behavior, 27*, 523–540. http://dx.doi.org/10.1023/A:1025438223608

Sternberg, K. J., Lamb, M. E., Esplin, P. W., Orbach, Y., & Hershkowitz, I. (2002). Using a structure interview protocol to improve the quality of investigative interviews. In L. M. Mitchell, J. A. Quas, & G. S. Goodman (Eds.), *Memory and suggestibility in the forensic interview* (pp. 409–436). Mahwah, NJ: Erlbaum.

Sternberg, K. J., Lamb, M. E., Orbach, Y., Esplin, P. W., & Mitchell, S. (2001). Use of a structured investigative protocol enhances young children's responses to free-recall prompts in the course of forensic interviews. *Journal of Applied Psychology, 86*, 997–1005. http://dx.doi.org/10.1037/0021-9010.86.5.997

Stovall v. Denno, 388 U.S. 293 (1967).

Tanaka, J. W., & Farah, M. J. (1993). Parts and wholes in face recognition. *Quarterly Journal of Experimental Psychology, 46*, 225–245. http://dx.doi.org/10.1080/14640749308401045

United States of America v. Mitchell, Case No. 2:08CR125DAK (2010).

U.S. Department of Health & Human Services. (2013). *Child maltreatment.* Retrieved from http://www.acf.hhs.gov/sites/default/files/cb/cm2013.pdf

Wagstaff, G. F., MacVeigh, J., Boston, R., Scott, L., Brunas-Wagstaff, J., & Cole, J. (2003). Can laboratory findings on eyewitness testimony be generalized to the real world? An archival analysis of the influence of violence, weapon presence, and age on eyewitness accuracy. *Journal of Psychology: Interdisciplinary and Applied, 137*, 17–28. http://dx.doi.org/10.1080/00223980309600596

Ward, C. (2012, September 14). Former neighbor guilty of killing girl, 7, in 1957. *Chicago Tribune News.* Retrieved from http://articles.chicagotribune.com/2012-09-14/news/chi-mccullough-guilty-of-killing-girl-7-in-1957-20120914_1_ridulph-case-ralph-tessier-sycamore-girl

Ward, C. (2015, February 13). Court upholds conviction in 1957 murder of 7-year-old Sycamore girl. *Chicago Tribune.* Retrieved from http://www.

chicagotribune.com/news/local/breaking/ct-mccullough-appeal-met-0214-20150213-story.html

Waterman, A. H., Blades, M., & Spencer, C. (2004). Indicating when you do not know the answer: The effect of question format and interviewer knowledge on children's "don't know" responses. *British Journal of Developmental Psychology, 22*, 335–348. http://dx.doi.org/10.1348/0261510041552710

Wells, G. L. (1978). Applied eyewitness testimony research: System variables and estimator variables. *Journal of Personality and Social Psychology, 36*, 1546–1557. http://dx.doi.org/10.1037/0022-3514.36.12.1546

Wells, G. L. (1984). Verbal descriptions of faces from memory: Are they diagnostic of identification accuracy? *Journal of Applied Psychology, 70*, 619–626. http://dx.doi.org/10.1037/0021-9010.70.4.619

Wells, G. L. (1993). What do we know about eyewitness identification? *American Psychologist, 48*, 553–571. http://dx.doi.org/10.1037/0003-066X.48.5.553

Wells, G. L., & Hryciw, B. (1984). Memory for faces: Encoding and retrieval operations. *Memory & Cognition, 12*, 338–344. http://dx.doi.org/10.3758/BF03198293

Wells, G. L., Leippe, M. R., & Ostrom, T. M. (1979). Guidelines for empirically assessing the fairness of a lineup. *Law and Human Behavior, 3*, 285–293. http://dx.doi.org/10.1007/BF01039807

Wells, G. L., & Lindsay, R. C. (1980). On estimating the diagnosticity of eyewitness nonidentifications. *Psychological Bulletin, 88*, 776–784. http://dx.doi.org/10.1037/0033-2909.88.3.776

Wells, G. L., & Luus, C. A. E. (1990). Police lineups as experiments: Social methodology as a framework for properly conducted lineups. *Personality and Social Psychology Bulletin, 16*, 106–117. http://dx.doi.org/10.1177/0146167290161008

Wells, G. L., Malpass, R. S., Lindsay, R. C. L., Fisher, R. P., Turtle, J. W., & Fulero, S. M. (2000). From the lab to the police station: A successful application of eyewitness research. *American Psychologist, 55*, 581–598. http://dx.doi.org/10.1037/0003-066X.55.6.581

Wells, G. L., & Olson, E. A. (2003). Eyewitness testimony. *Annual Review of Psychology, 54*, 277–295. http://dx.doi.org/10.1146/annurev.psych.54.101601.145028

Wells, G. L., Rydell, S. M., & Seelau, E. P. (1993). The selection of distractors for eyewitness lineups. *Journal of Applied Psychology, 78*, 835–844. http://dx.doi.org/10.1037/0021-9010.78.5.835

Wells, G. L., Steblay, N. K., & Dysart, J. E. (2015). Double-blind photo lineups using actual eyewitnesses: An experimental test of a sequential versus simultaneous lineup procedure. *Law and Human Behavior, 39*, 1–14. http://dx.doi.org/10.1037/lhb0000096

Wells, G. L., & Turtle, J. W. (1986). Eyewitness identification: The importance of lineup models. *Psychological Bulletin, 99*, 320–329. http://dx.doi.org/10.1037/0033-2909.99.3.320

Wiese, H., Schweinberger, S. R., & Hansen, K. (2008). The age of the beholder: ERP evidence of an own-age bias in face memory. *Neuropsychologia, 46*, 2973–2985. http://dx.doi.org/10.1016/j.neuropsychologia.2008.06.007

Winograd, E. (1976). Recognition memory for faces following nine different judgments. *Bulletin of the Psychonomic Society, 8*, 419–421. http://dx.doi.org/10.3758/BF03335185

Wright, A. M., & Holliday, R. E. (2007). Enhancing the recall of young, young–old and old–old adults with cognitive interviews. *Applied Cognitive Psychology, 21*, 19–43. http://dx.doi.org/10.1002/acp.1260

Wright, D. B., Hanoteau, F., Parkinson, C., & Tatham, A. (2010). Perceptions about memory reliability and honesty for children of 3 to 18 years old. *Legal and Criminological Psychology, 15*, 195–207. http://dx.doi.org/10.1348/135532508X400347

Wright, D. B., & Loftus, E. F. (2008). Eyewitness memory. In G. Cohen & M. A. Conway (Eds.), *Memory in the real world* (3rd ed., pp. 91–105). New York, NY: Psychology Press.

Wright, D. B., & Stroud, J. N. (2002). Age differences in lineup identification accuracy: People are better with their own age. *Law and Human Behavior, 26*, 641–654. http://dx.doi.org/10.1023/A:1020981501383

Yarmey, A. D., Yarmey, M. J., & Yarmey, A. L. (1996). Accuracy of eyewitness identifications in showups and lineups. *Law and Human Behavior, 20*, 459–477. http://dx.doi.org/10.1007/BF01498981

Yerkes, R. M., & Dodson, J. D. (1908). The relationship of strength of stimulus to rapidity of habit formation. *Journal of Comparative Neurology and Psychology, 18*, 459–482.

Yuille, J. C., Hunter, R., Joffe, R., & Zaparniuk, J. (1993). Interviewing children in sexual abuse cases. In G. S. Goodman & B. L. Bottoms (Eds.), *Child victims, child witnesses* (pp. 95–115). New York, NY: Guilford Press.

Zajac, R., & Jack, F. (2015). Improving children's performance on photographic lineups: Do the physical properties of a 'wildcard' make a difference? *Legal and Criminological Psychology.* http://dx.doi.org/10.1111/lcrp.12075

Zajac, R., & Karageorge, A. (2009). The wildcard: A simple technique for improving children's target-absent lineup performance. *Applied Cognitive Psychology, 23*, 358–368. http://dx.doi.org/10.1002/acp.1511

Index

About the Author

Joanna Pozzulo, PhD, is a professor of psychology and chair of the Department of Psychology at Carleton University, Ottawa, Ontario, Canada. Dr. Pozzulo is a leading expert on children's eyewitness identification abilities. Her research, funded by the Social Sciences and Humanities Research Council and Carleton University, focuses on the development of face memory and the procedures that police can use to increase the reliability of eyewitness identification from lineups. Dr. Pozzulo has coauthored two textbooks on forensic psychology. She has received numerous awards for her research and teaching.